ACPL ITEM
DISCARDED

Th...   om-
bir...   e of
doctors and child psychologists, and the actual day-to-day experiences of parents like you. Covering a wide variety of subjects, these books answer all your questions, step by important step, and provide the confidence of knowing you're doing the best for your child—with help from *Parents*™ Magazine.

D1554343

Parents™
Book of
Child Safety

DAVID LASKIN

BALLANTINE BOOKS • NEW YORK

The advice in this book is intended to acquaint you with basic safety precautions and to help you deal with a variety of emergency situations until medical help can be obtained. It is in no way intended as a substitute for professional medical counseling. If your child has a special medical condition, you should ask your doctor whether you should take any special precautions.

Sale of this book without a front cover may be unauthorized. If this book is coverless, it may have been reported to the publisher as "unsold or destroyed" and neither the author nor the publisher may have received payment for it.

Copyright © 1991 by Gruner and Jahr USA, Publishing

All rights reserved under International and Pan-American Copyright Conventions. Published in the United States of America by Ballantine Books, a division of Random House, Inc., New York, and simultaneously in Canada by Random House of Canada Limited, Toronto.

Library of Congress Catalog Card Number: 91-92104

ISBN 0-345-35104-5

Manufactured in the United States of America

First Edition: December 1991

The illustrations of CPR techniques on pages 256 to 264 appear courtesy of the American Red Cross.

Illustrations by Ray Skibinski and Bob Deschamps.

Contents

Part Three

Testing the Waters: *The Preschool Years, Ages Three to Five*

Part Four

Out in the World: *The Early School Years, Ages Five to Seven*

Acknowledgments

My first thanks go to all the parents who shared with me their wisdom, their safety tips, their experiences, and their anecdotes about keeping their children safe.

I would also like to thank the following individuals in fields connected to child safety and child welfare who answered my questions and made available the resources of their organizations: Katie Bond, information specialist with the American Humane Association; Dean W. Childs, director of Traffic Safety Services of the American Automobile Association; Joyce Coonley of the U.S. Consumer Products Safety Commission; Bob Hall of Parents Anonymous of Delaware; Jan Kirby-Gell, sexual-abuse specialist with the National Center on Child Abuse and Neglect; Joseph Greensher, M.D., Associate Chairman, Department of Pediatrics, at Winthrop-University Hospital in New York; Shirley Maag of the National Organization of the Mothers of Twins Club; Cindy Moelis, research analyst with the National Committee for the Prevention of Child Abuse; Ramona Redding of the National Safety Council; Patricia A. Toth, director of the National

Center for the Prosecution of Child Abuse; the staff of the C. Henry Kempe National Center for the Prevention and Treatment of Child Abuse and Neglect; the staff of Child Find of America, Inc.; the staff of the National Center for Missing and Exploited Children.

My continuing gratitude to Elizabeth Crow at *Parents* and to Virginia Faber at Ballantine for their help and guidance on this and other projects.

And a special thank you to my children, Emily, Sarah, and Alice, for giving me a total immersion in all aspects of child safety and to my wife, Kathleen O'Neill, for helping to keep us all safe and happy.

Introduction: A Safer Childhood for Our Children

Safety is a concern that arrives full-blown on the day we become parents. All at once we have a tiny, precious, helpless bundle of awesome responsibility to care for. How are we going to feed and clothe the new baby? How are we going to get her home from the hospital? Where is she going to sleep? What is she going to play with? These are some of the first safety questions that spring to mind—and many hundreds of others are quick to follow, crowding in on us ever thicker and ever thornier as our newborns catapult themselves through babyhood and childhood. Keeping the six-month-old from rolling off the changing table seems like a snap when we're chasing after a sixteen-month-old who is determined to topple down the steps; keeping an ingenious, nimble preschooler from escaping from the yard makes toddler safety look straight-forward; and then all of these early childhood safety issues pale beside the *real* worries of keeping our school-age children safe in the world "out there." Dealing with strangers, child molesters, the school bus, camping trips,

1

swimming pools, peer pressure . . . the list goes on and on until even the heartiest parent can feel a bit daunted.

Don't be overwhelmed. But do be aware. There is no getting around the vital importance of safety, no matter what stage of development our children have reached. The fact is that more children die in America from accidents than from disease. Each year, some 26 million children under the age of sixteen sustain injuries in accidents and well over 7000 children die in car accidents, fires, from drowning, poisoning, choking, and falls. Children under the age of fifteen account for about one-third of all pedestrian deaths and injuries. More than 100,000 children a year are victims of child sexual abuse. And the U.S. Department of Justice estimates that the number of children who were abducted in 1988 may be as high as 358,700. Many, many of these accidents could have been prevented—by us, by our children, by both of us working together. Many children could have been spared the nightmare of sexual abuse if we had been informed and had taken the time to inform them and to listen to them. Many children might have been safe from kidnappers if the proper precautions were taken.

That is what *The Parents Book of Child Safety* is all about. Giving parents the information they need to prevent accidents; helping parents give children the skills and the confidence to protect themselves from accidents, from abuse, and abduction. The book is divided into four sections covering the four periods that a child passes through in the first seven years of life: babyhood, from birth to eighteen months; the toddler years, from eighteen months to three years; the preschool years, from three to five; and the early school years, from five to seven. Each section addresses the special safety concerns that arise during this period of development. All sections contain both practical tips for how to insure safety on a day-to-day, activity-by-activity, room-by-room basis and discussions of how to instill safe habits and attitudes in the growing child.

Although child safety may strike some parents as a scary subject, *The Parents' Book of Child Safety* is *not* a scary book. Quite the contrary, it is a very reassuring book. It is a book of success stories, not horror stories; a book of accidents that don't have to happen and that *won't* happen if we have the foresight and awareness to prevent them. The parents I interviewed for the book have kept their children safe by devoting that extra bit of time and effort to looking after them, talking with them, practicing with them. They learned from their mistakes, and some of them have just been lucky. Marge's preschooler *was* found by the police when he wandered a mile from home; Victoria's early school-age son was *not* abducted when he agreed to go for a ride with a lady who said she knew his mother; Mary's toddler only suffered a small bruise when he ran into the sharp, uncovered edge of the coffee table; my infant daughter did *not* poke out her eye when she miraculously jumped halfway across the living room in three seconds flat to grab an open diaper pin. There were valuable lessons in all of these near misses; and you can profit from our mistakes and our good fortune.

You can also profit from the advice that experienced parents dispensed on a wide range of safety issues. One excellent piece of advice that I heard over and over again was: it's never too soon to begin discussing safety with children. Babies too young to talk can understand when you tell them something is a "No." Toddlers, though they may not always obey, do listen and understand much more than they let on. Preschoolers demand to know the reason *why* for everything we tell them or ask them; this can be an exasperating trait, but when it comes to safety discussions they are perfectly justified. By helping our children understand the reason for safety rules now, we are equipping them to make safe choices and adopt safe habits later when they are on their own. Lectures, ultimatums, even non physical punishment may be necessary sometimes; but in the long run, open discussions—the more specific, low-key, and reassuring the better—are the most effective way of getting the safety message across. Each section of the book contains detailed guidelines on how to discuss safety and what safety issues to discuss.

Since common sense is at the heart of so many safety matters, this book takes a common sense approach in its organization. Within the four chronologically arranged sections, individual chapters follow a child geographically as he moves into an ever-widening world. Chapters in the section on babies cover all the basic supplies and equipment parents need for safe infant care, explain how to use these safely in the routines of day-to-day care, and then detail everything parents need to know about baby proofing. In the toddler section we move out into the world of play equipment, yards, wading pools, playgrounds, and all the new things a toddler can do (and new trouble he can get into) around the house. Books, songs, and games are ideal ways of introducing toddlers to the topic of safety and of quelling some of the fears that come up at this time.

With preschool children we enter the realm of safety away from home—in day-care centers and play schools. This section also contains an in-depth chapter on child sexual abuse, useful for parents with children of any age.

The final section, on the early school years, stresses the importance of a continuing dialogue on safety between parent and child and looks at the new safety issues that come up as five-to-seven-year-olds assume more responsibility for their own care. There are tips on getting children to school safely and discussions of how to prepare children in this age group for encounters with strangers and potential abductors. These children are not only out in the world of school, but actively participating in sports, camping trips, family vacations, and perhaps even traveling unaccompanied on airplanes or buses—and there is information on safety essentials in each of these situations.

Just as a child's physical world expands as she develops, so do her psychological and intellectual worlds. Obviously we all want our children to be aware of the hazards around them, whether these hazards are speeding cars, household poisons, or child molesters; but we don't want them to be *so aware* of hazards that they grow up timid, suspicious, and perpetually frightened of taking new steps on their own. Finding the balance between preserving the blessed innocence of childhood and preparing children for the sometimes harsh reality of the world is a major challenge for parents today. *The Parents' Book of Child Safety* addresses this challenge with practical, workable advice appropriate to children in all four age groups. The book takes into account our children's individual differences in personality, interests, fears, and emotional needs as well as the different safety issues that arise in cities, suburbs, country, or farm settings.

Since, despite all our precautions, preparations, and discussions, accidents *do* sometimes happen, *The Parents' Book of Child Safety* contains a special section on how to deal quickly and competently with the most common emergencies. This section, entitled *In Case of Emergency*, begins on page ten.

Much as we love our children when they're young and much as we enjoy looking after them and taking care of them (at least *most* of the time), they do inevitably grow up, cease to be children, and start to take care of themselves. One of our goals as parents is to see that they take care of themselves safely—with not only awareness of the potential hazards of the world, but the ability and judgment to avoid these hazards, even ones we *haven't* discussed with them. As our little ones bound into adolescence and maturity, they will be facing evertougher pressures with ever-greater independence. Drugs and alcohol; safety behind the wheel; sexual awareness and responsibility in an era of deadly sexually transmitted diseases. These are a few of the safety issues that lie ahead. The foundations for their safe habits and attitudes in the future are being laid now—with the way we handle the baby who crawls toward the stove, the way we talk to the four-year-old who wants to know *why* he can't accept presents from someone he doesn't know, the explanation we give the nine-year-old who wants to go downtown alone because "everyone is doing it."

The span of time that separates the crawling baby from the driving teenager may seem infinitely long—or appallingly short—depending on how we look at it. But no matter what our perspective is, we all feel that these childhood years are a magical time for us and for our children. This is a book to help us and our children experience the magic together, safely and happily.

Part One

A Safe Beginning: The Baby Years, Birth to Eighteen Months

1. Preparing For the New Arrival

There's probably no event in life that calls up as many and as complicated emotions as the arrival of a new baby. Joy and pride are feelings we all expect to have, but nearly as powerful for many of us are feelings of anxiety, worry, and massive responsibility. We now have someone to care for in every sense of the word—and one of the most important aspects of that care is keeping the new baby safe.

Infant safety begins even *before* the hospital nurse hands you the baby at the hospital door and tells you, "She's yours now!" Infant safety begins as soon as you start shopping for the equipment necessary for infant care. Since equipment is part of nearly every activity you do with your baby—from dressing her to transporting her to putting her to sleep—it's essential to have the safest equipment you can get. This doesn't necessarily mean the most expensive. Nor does it mean that safe equipment alone is going to keep your baby safe: even the most reliable equipment is only as safe as the care giver using it.

Instinct and common sense will take you a good part

of the way to safe infant care, but there is also a certain amount of essential knowledge and information you should have. This chapter covers all the basic information on buying safe infant-care equipment and using it safely. When making your purchases, it's good to keep in mind as a general rule that *safety should come first*, before style, color, convenience, or any other consideration.

Car Seats

If you own a car, you must own a car seat for your infant—in fact, for *all* your children under forty pounds. Once they're over forty pounds, they should use seat belts. In all states car seats are required by law for babies and young children—and thus it's illegal even to drive your newborn home from the hospital without a car seat. Perhaps even more persuasive than laws are the statistics. Automobile accidents are the leading cause of death and injury to children and those who suffer the highest passenger death rate are infants under six months old. According to the National Safety Council, in 1986, 1100 children under four died from injuries sustained in car accidents and 50,000 children were injured. It is estimated that the majority of these deaths might have been prevented if some sort of restraint was used.

So the question is not *whether* to have a car seat, but *what kind*—and the answer is fairly simple. In 1981 strict federal regulations concerning children's car seats went into effect, and this means that *all* car seats manufactured after 1981 must meet certain basic safety standards. (A label on the seat carries the date of manufacture: check to make sure this date is *after* January 1, 1981.) There are two types of car seats appropriate for an infant (defined for purposes of car seats as a baby weighing twenty pounds or less): an infant seat or a convertible seat [illustrate both].

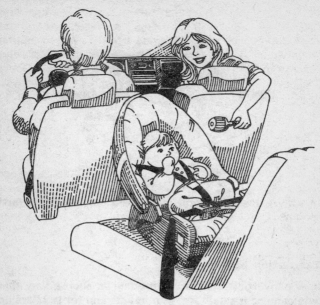

A properly installed infant car seat faces the rear of the car.

Infant Seat:

An infant car seat is rather like a molded tub that you strap into the backseat of your car with a seat belt. The seat itself is designed so that the baby is lying in a semi-reclining position and it has a shoulder harness that you fit around the baby and buckle up to keep him securely in place. A baby in a properly installed infant car seat will be facing the rear of the car: this is the only safe way for a baby to ride. The reason for this is that in case of an accident, the pressure of impact will be evenly distributed along the baby's back, not on his fragile chest and abdomen.

A convertible car seat for infants and toddlers under forty pounds.

Convertible Seat:

A convertible seat is constructed in such a way that you can use it safely for both infants and for toddlers up to forty pounds. When you're using it for an infant, you tilt it back into the semi-reclining position and install it in your car so that the child faces backward. For a toddler you make the seat upright, reverse it so that the child faces forward, and raise the straps to the next set of strap holes.

Which Is Better?

As far as safety goes, it really doesn't matter so long as you use the seat *every time you drive with your baby* and so long as you use it correctly. Thus, the safest seat is the seat you consistently and correctly use. As far as convenience goes, the infant seat has the advantage that you can remove the seat with your baby in it easily, thus avoiding waking the baby up when you reach your destination. An infant car seat can also double as an infant seat you use around the house. (The reverse, however, is not true so be careful that you don't try to use a standard infant seat in the car. The two may look alike, but only a seat specifically designed for car safety will provide the proper restraint in the car.) On the other hand, a convertible seat will unquestionably save you money since you'll be purchasing only one single seat that will serve through the early childhood years. However, some convertible car seats are really too big for small babies and will only work comfortably if you buy a special insert or if you prop the baby up with rolled blankets.

Remember Face Back Only:

No matter whether you use an infant seat or convertible seat for your newborn, the seat *must* be installed in the rear-facing position. When your baby reaches twenty pounds, you may turn a convertible seat to face forward or graduate him from his infant seat to a toddler seat (see Chapter 4). If your baby seems to like (or tolerate) facing backward in his convertible seat, leave it that way. The rear-facing position is the safer position.

Use the Seat for Every Car Trip:

No matter how short the trip or how slowly you're moving, your baby should be securely buckled into her car seat every time she travels in the car. If she fusses, make frequent stops or bring things for her to look at. An infant who has become accustomed to riding in a car seat will be less resistant to using the seat through the early childhood years. In fact, a toddler may refuse to ride in the car unless she's properly strapped into her seat.

Tips for Buying and Using Car Seats:

• Always read and follow the instructions provided for the car seat. Installation and strapping procedures may differ for different seats.

- Buy a car seat that is comfortable for your baby, easy for you to get the baby in and out of, and easy to install and remove from your car. Test it out in the store if possible.
- Avoid convertible seats that require the installation of a tether attachment in your car. These can be difficult to install properly, but if they are not installed correctly the seat will not be safe.
- Make sure the seat will fit in your car(s), that it doesn't block the rearview mirror, and that if you have more than one young child, the car will hold as many car seats as you need.
- Make sure harness straps are adjusted so that they're snug but not too tight. You'll have to loosen and readjust them as the baby grows and also seasonally depending on the bulk of your baby's clothing.
- Check the seat belt holding the car seat in place periodically to make sure it hasn't loosened up.
- The safest position for the car seat is in the middle of the car's backseat. The least safe place is the front seat next to the right window.
- Buy a seat that is easy to clean.
- If the car is parked in the sun, any plastic, metal, or chrome section of the seat can quickly become hot enough to burn a baby. Cover the seat with a blanket or towel whenever you park in a sunny spot.
- If you haven't had time to buy a car seat, check to see if you can rent one from the hospital. You might also be able to get one through a loaner program.
- When renting a car, always check ahead to reserve the proper type of seat.
- Never use a car seat that has been in a car involved in a serious accident. The impact of collision may well have damaged or weakened the structure of the seat, making it unsafe for continued use.

Crib slats should be set no more than 2 ⅜" apart; no more than two adult fingers should be able to fit between mattress and crib.

Cribs

A crib is likely to be the single most expensive piece of equipment you buy for your newborn and it's also likely to be the one you use the most, so you want to be sure you get one that is safe and well made. In 1973 the federal government made buying a safe crib a little easier for parents by enacting certain regulations on crib manufacture: crib slats must not be set farther apart than 2⅜ inches; crib mattress must not be more than 5 inches thick; crib mattress must fit inside crib so that no more than two adult fingers may be placed between mattress and side of crib.

These are the basics of crib safety and, when shopping for a crib, you should look for a label on the crib indicating that it has been made according to these federal standards. However, these standards alone are not a guarantee of safety: first because they do not cover all aspects of crib design and structure, and second because they provide no guidance on safe crib use. Even after the federal regulations went into effect, cribs (and crib-related equipment including mattresses and crib toys) continue to be related to more infant deaths than any other piece of baby equipment. So it's essential that parents exercise some caution in buying a crib and crib accessories and that they follow certain rules in using and maintaining the crib safely.

Tips for Buying Crib

- *Stability* is essential in a safe crib. Check headboards, frame, and mattress support for strength. Best are cribs that have steel stabilizing bars as part of the frame.
- *Corner posts:* should be avoided; if you do buy a crib with this design, make sure the posts are less than ⅝ inch high. High corner posts, headboards with curving designs set near crib corners, or headboards with decorative openings are a hazard because the baby could get his head caught or loop a piece of clothing or dangling string, necklace, or pacifier cord around the post and strangle. (Pacifier cords and necklaces are a hazard in themselves: better the baby cries than have his pacifier attached to him by a cord around his neck.)
- *Drop sides:* should still come up at least four inches above the mattress even when lowered. Though you would never leave the baby alone in the crib with the sides down, it's still better to have this extra margin of safety.

- *Graduated mattress support hooks*: allow you to lower the mattress as the baby grows. Once the baby can stand, you'll want the mattress to be as deep in the crib as possible to make it difficult for the baby to climb out.
- *Plastic teething guard*: will prevent the baby from chewing on the top rail of the crib and getting splinters or swallowing paint.

Tips for Using Crib and Crib Accessories:

- *Sides up*: Whenever the baby is in his crib, the drop sides should be locked in place. Check to see that the lock has caught.
- *Check hardware*: The screws and bolts that hold the crib together may become loosened with use (or may have been insufficiently tightened by the installer): check all the connections before beginning to use the crib and periodically thereafter.
- *Check mattress hangers*: Before using the crib, make sure all four mattress hangers are securely in place in the mattress support hooks at the same level. Whenever you move the crib or the mattress, check the mattress hangers again. As your baby grows, lower the mattress.
- *Crib placement*: Make sure the crib is well away from drape or blind cords that a child could place around his neck, radiators he might touch, space heaters he might throw his blankets onto, or hazardous objects he might reach. Never use the crib corner posts to hang strings (for example, a string-tie laundry or shopping bag; marionettes), rubber bands, ribbons.
- *Bumpers*: will protect an infant's head from banging against the bars of the crib. Bumpers should entirely surround the inside of the crib, tie or snap into place in six places (cut off long tie strings). Make sure all the bumper ties or snaps are fastened at all times. Plastic bumpers are easier to clean, but your baby may chew them apart and get at the filling: remove and replace the bumpers as soon as this happens. Also hard plastic

bumpers give babies more of a boost when they begin climbing, so soft bumpers are preferable overall.

- *Safe sheets*: Do not use plastic sheets or thin plastic bags as mattress covers—the baby could suffocate. Protect the mattress with special rubberized sheets made for this purpose.
- *Safe toys and pillows*: Do not put pillows or large stuffed animals in the crib—these could smother the baby. Safe crib toys are soft, too large to be swallowed, durable enough not to be chewed to pieces, devoid of string or elastic on which the baby could strangle, are nontoxic and have no sharp edges or small removable parts (e.g., buttons, glass eyes in stuffed animals). Well before your baby can sit or stand (as early as five months), remove any crib toys, such as crib gyms or hanging objects that have elastic or dangling string, on which the baby could strangle. Infant books in cloth or plastic, safety mirrors (plastic with steel borders) and colorful cloth balls are good choices. When your baby begins climbing, remove any crib toys that he could stack and use as a ladder to climb out of his crib.
- *Mobiles*: are safe only until the baby can pull himself to a stand. Then they should be removed

Used Cribs:

Are fine, so long as they meet the safety guidelines described above. Check carefully for splinters, cracked or peeling paint. When refinishing the crib, make sure you use household enamel paint made after February 1978: earlier paints could have high lead content. If you suspect the crib's original paint has high lead content, strip it off and repaint the crib. High corner posts can be unscrewed or cut off, sanded down, and repainted.

Other Nursery Furniture

Changing Tables:

Though not strictly necessary for infant care, changing tables are a great convenience and a great preventer of parental backaches. They do, however, present one obvious hazard: a baby can fall off. In the past ten years, nine babies died by falling from their changing tables and, according to the Consumer Products Safety Commission, about 1400 babies each year must be taken to hospital emergency rooms because of injuries related to falls from changing tables.

To prevent falls, try to find a changing table with a restraining strap, but *do not rely on the strap alone* to keep the child safe. The strap will permit you to turn your back or reach for a clean diaper, but it will not hold the child securely or reliably enough for you to leave the room. Safest is to use a strap and keep hand contact with the baby on the table.

Make sure the changing table is stable and not placed in such a way that an older baby could topple it over by kicking against the wall or another piece of furniture.

Keep powders, ointments, pins, premoistened wipes, etc., out of the baby's reach. A national survey of poison-control centers found that 2 percent of poisonings reportedly occurred during diaper changes.

Toy Chests:

Are not a hazard to newborns, but may be hazardous once the baby can pull himself up to a stand. The Consumer Products Safety Commission reports that in 1989 approximately 3600 children under age four required hos-

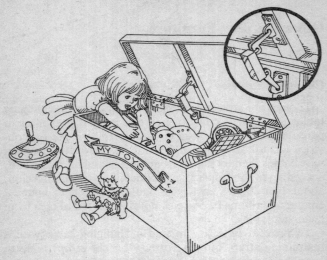

A toy chest with a safety support keeps the lid open to whatever position the child pushes it.

pital emergency-room treatment from injuries related to toy chests and boxes—in some cases children suffered serious brain damage when toy chest lids fell on their heads. Children have also suffocated by closing themselves into airtight toy chests. The easiest way to avoid these dangers is to buy (or make) a toy chest without a lid or to remove the lid of the chest. If you do buy a chest with a hinged lid, you can get one with a safety support that keeps the lid open to whatever position your child pushes it. Also, make sure the chest has air holes and that there are no locks or latches that could close your child in. Check the lid safety support from time to time to see that it's working properly and firmly set in place.

If you have any doubt about the safety of the toy chest lid, remove it.

Infant Seats:

Parents like infant seats made of molded (and often padded) plastic because of the convenience they provide for feeding and "parking" babies, and babies like them because they can sit up and be a part of the action around them. But you must take care when using these seats: even small, seemingly immobile babies can topple their seats off the edges of tables or counters by pushing off with their feet, and they can easily fall or slide out of the seats.

When buying and using an infant seat, make sure you get a sturdy, stable model with nonskid feet; only buy one with restraining crotch and waist straps and make sure you use these straps each time you put the baby in the seat; even if the baby is safely strapped in, never leave him alone in the seat: a fall off a slippery table could occur while your back is turned. Two more "nevers": never put an infant seat near the edge of a counter, table, or other high surface; never use an infant seat as a car seat. (Many models *look* like infant car seats but they lack the proper design to keep the baby safe in the car—see car seats above.)

Some experts caution parents against leaving babies in infant seats too long: the seats do not hold a baby in a natural position and a baby given bottles only in a seat lacks the physical closeness and affection that all babies crave.

Playpens:

Playpens, like infant seats, are a nice convenience for parents and a comfortable place for a baby to play—so long as he is not left there too much. A baby who spends a large part of his day in a playpen will miss out on the physical contact he needs most.

Some of the makers of playpens have agreed to comply

with certain regulations and standards in the manufacture of this product, and playpens that accord with the standards will carry a seal of certification by the Juvenile Products Manufacturers Association. Make sure any playpen you purchase carries this seal.

Also, be certain that the slats of wooden playpens are not set more than 2⅜ inches apart (a bigger space would allow a child to get his head caught between the slats) and that the netting of mesh playpens has a small weave so buttons on clothing do not catch in it. Mesh-sided playpens pose a serious hazard if their drop sides are left down: children have suffocated when they rolled or slipped into the pocket of mesh that forms when the side is down. This is not a defect in the product, but in the way the product is used. When setting up mesh playpens, *make sure you always raise the side up all the way and lock it securely in place*. Inspect the playpen hardware periodically to make sure it's working properly and repair any tears in the fabric, the mat, and especially the padding or covering on the top rail at once.

Bookshelves:

Bookshelves for the nursery should be sturdy enough so that the baby can't pull them over on top of herself, free of splinters or paint chips, and of course, painted with lead-free paint.

Walkers:

Today more and more pediatricians and child-safety experts are discouraging the use of walkers. A baby in a walker can reach things that a crawling or standing baby could not reach, he can travel all over the house at very fast speeds, and he is at serious risk if the walker topples over (a common occurrence on door thresholds, bumpy rugs, or when traveling from a rug to a hard floor), or if he falls down the stairs in his walker. Babies have also caught their fingers in the hinges or when walkers accidentally collapse. The Consumer Products Safety Commission estimates that in 1989 over 20,000 children from birth to age four were injured in accidents related to walkers or jumpers.

If, despite these hazards, you decide to use a walker, make sure you attend the baby when he's in it. Avoid using the walker on uneven surfaces or outdoors and never carry the walker when the baby is in it.

Clothes

Safe baby clothes are flame-retardant, nonbinding, and devoid of ornaments that a baby could swallow, strangle on, get tangled up in, chew off, or get cut by. Flame-retardant clothing is especially important for the outfits your baby sleeps in (though you probably won't distinguish between sleepwear and playwear for a newborn). Flame-retardant does not mean fireproof: it means the clothing will cease burning when it is no longer exposed to fire. Many laundry detergents, including those specifically manufactured for baby clothes, will wash the flame-retardant property out of the clothes. Check the labels on the detergent box before washing baby clothes. The Consumer Products Safety Commission has a requirement that all children's sleepwear (up to and including size 14) must be manufactured from flame-retardant cloth.

Cotton clothing, though soft, does burn. Wool is warmer than acrylic, but most babies' skin is too delicate to have wool right next to it.

Carriers, Strollers, and Carriages

Babies need and love to be held, hugged, carried in one's arms, and cuddled close, but when it comes to outings, a stroller or carrier is a tremendous advantage. You gain the safety of protecting the baby from being dropped in case you fall or trip and the convenience of having your arms or hands free. Rare indeed is the baby who doesn't come to adore her outings in a front carrier, backpack, or stroller or the parent who doesn't come to depend on one to get through the week.

Until your baby can hold her head up, she should only be taken out in a front carrier, a stroller in the fully reclining position or a carriage. The popular and convenient umbrella strollers are great, but since these do not recline all the way to a flat position, you should hold off using them until the baby has the muscle power to support her head, usually at about three months.

Front Carriers

For newborns, front carriers are often the best and safest bet. Straps go over your shoulders and around your waist and soft cloth holds the baby next to your middle. When buying a front carrier, look for one that gives the baby good neck and head support, that has arm and leg holes big enough not to pinch or cut off circulation, but not so big that the baby will fall through, that is washable and made of a material suitable to your climate. For your own comfort and convenience, get a front carrier with adjustable, padded shoulder straps and make sure you can get your baby into and out of it unassisted.

Backpacks

Babies grow fast and when they become too big and heavy for a front carrier, you might want to switch to a backpack for outings. Remember, however, that *no baby should be carried in a backpack until he can hold his head up quite steadily on his own and has good muscle tone in his neck and shoulders*. This usually comes around four

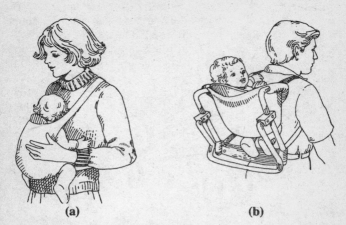

(a) **(b)**

(a) Front carriers are the best and safest bet for newborns.
(b) Use back packs as baby gets bigger and heavier (four to five months). They should not be used until baby can hold up his head.

to five months. Babies put in backpacks too young will flop over and the jolts they receive as you walk could damage their necks.

Like a front carrier, a back carrier should have leg openings large enough not to pinch and small enough so that the baby doesn't slip through. The carrier's metal frame should be padded, especially in the part near the baby's face, and the frame should have no hinges or joints in which the baby's fingers could get pinched. With some backpacks you really must struggle to put them on and take them off by yourself: so try it out in the store before you buy one. Look for packs that stand up by themselves, so you can get the baby all strapped in before hoisting him onto your back.

When using a backpack, make sure you always bend from the knee: if you bend from the waist, the baby could fall out, even if he's belted in. Since you can't see what

An umbrella stroller is convenient once the baby can hold up his head (about three months).

the baby is doing (or what is being done to him) in a backpack, you might think twice about using one in a crowded street or subway, in a store full of delicate objects, or on a hiking trail on which the baby could grab poisonous berries or leaves. (In any case, when taking the baby on the trail, it's safer to hike with another adult, and your companion could keep an eye on what the baby is up to.) If the pack has a stand, never leave the baby alone in the pack while it's standing.

Strollers and Carriages

For most of us with young children, a stroller is nearly as useful for outings as our shoes. From the time our babies reach about three months until they're about three, strollers make outings of all kinds easier. Carriages do have a certain old-fashioned charm and they are a comfortable, warm way to transport newborns who can't hold their heads up yet, but they tend to be much more cumbersome and expensive than strollers and useful for a much shorter period. Once a baby can sit up or pull himself up, he's safer in a stroller.

In 1983, the Juvenile Products Manufacturers Association adopted certain regulations for the safety of strollers and carriages. These include: no sharp edges, a locking device to insure that the stroller cannot be folded with a baby in it, a safety restraining strap, effective brakes, stability, adequate instructions and directions. If the stroller or carriage satisfies these requirements, the product will carry a certification seal of the JPMA. Look for this seal before making your purchase. Beyond this, there are a number of other safety measures you should be aware of:

Tips for Buying and Using Strollers and Carriages:

- *Stability:* The stroller should not tip when the child leans over the side or when you recline the seat back.
- *Shopping-basket attachment on stroller*: should be positioned low down on the back of the stroller and either in front of or right over the rear axle.
- *Seat strap*: is a must any time you use the stroller. Make sure the belt attachments are durable and easy to fasten.
- *Brake action*: Test in the store to make certain brakes really do lock stroller wheels.
- *Hanging articles off back of stroller*: is a hazard because the stroller could tip backward. Either carry pocketbooks, shopping bags, etc., yourself or use the shopping-basket attachment.
- *When folding stroller*: always make certain that your child's fingers are well clear of the hinges.
- *Carriage body secure to frame*: Make sure the basket section of the carriage locks or snaps securely onto the carriage frame.

- *No standing in stroller or carriage* : Not a concern with a newborn, but a real hazard later on.
- *Always attend baby*: Whether in a stroller or a carriage, a baby must never be left alone outside the home.

Toys

Newborn babies love toys they can look at, particularly those with faces, and older babies are great explorers of texture, shape, size, and especially taste. You can be absolutely certain that a six-month-old will grab everything within his reach and bring it right to his mouth. That's why it's essential that you choose your baby's toys with some care. The guiding rules in toy selection are:

- Toys must be large enough so that they cannot be swallowed or lodge in a baby's throat.
- They must be nontoxic.
- They must have no small parts that could break or be chewed off.
- They must be soft enough not to hurt a baby if she rolls over on them.
- They must have no jagged edges or splinters.
- They must have no dangling strings or connective elastic that a baby could strangle on.

Remember: Toy manufacturers are not always as careful as they should be in designing toys, and government agencies sometimes lag in their toy recalls. The Consumer Products Safety Commission reports that toys were related to 35 deaths in 1986 and 100,000 injuries serious enough to require hospitalization. It's up to you to assess the safety and suitability of the toys you buy and receive. Be especially careful with imported toys (including crayons, finger paints, markers) as many foreign countries are far less careful than the U.S. in regulating toy manufacture for safety.

If you have any doubts about the safety of a toy, call the Consumer Products Safety Commission hotline at: 1–800–638–CPSC. This office has a staff of workers whose job it is to test toys for safety. Sometimes an unsafe toy can be made safe if you throw out a single piece or sew together certain parts. This office will give you full instructions and provide the latest information on toy recalls. You can also obtain a booklet (one for children from birth to age five, another for kids from six to twelve) entitled *Which Toy for Which Child* by writing to:

> Consumer Products Safety Commission
> Washington, D.C. 20207

Mobiles and Crib Gyms

Newborns spend a good deal of time lying in their cribs and so crib toys such as mobiles or crib gyms are favorites for them. These toys are safe only so long as your baby cannot reach them: as soon as he can get up on his hands and knees or begin to pull up on the bars of his crib, these toys should be removed from the crib. During the early months when crib gyms are still safe to use, check them from time to time to make sure they are installed properly.

Stuffed Animals

Stuffed animals with big, clearly outlined faces are great for babies, so long as they can't chew off the eyes or eat through to the stuffing. If you receive these toys as gifts, check them over carefully before letting your baby have them. Never put a large stuffed toy in a baby's crib because the baby could suffocate on it when young and use it to climb out later on.

Mirrors

A baby from about two to six months is fascinated by studying his reflection in a mirror and will enjoy having a mirror of his very own to play with. Of course the only mirror that is safe is a nonbreakable one made specially for babies. Look for plastic mirrors with steel borders. Many models attach easily to the inside of the baby's crib.

Rattles

Rattles are fine for a baby as long as they're large enough not to be lodged in the throat and durable enough not to splinter or crack. In fact, enough babies choked on rattles for the Consumer Products Safety Commission to mandate regulations about the size, shape, and construction of baby rattles. These regulations went into effect in August of 1978, so rattles made in the past thirteen years are okay. Even so, it makes good sense to check any rattle for small parts, to watch the baby as he mouthes the rattle to see if he can get it far back in his throat, and to take rattles out of the playpen and the crib when the baby is left alone.

Books

As soon as your baby can sit up in your lap, she will enjoy books—although at first she'll probably spend more time mouthing them than looking at them. Look for soft cloth books, plastic books, and laminated-cardboard baby books marked "nontoxic." Beware of so-called activity books with small parts that a child could chew or break off and swallow.

High Chairs and Hook-on Seats

Babies can start to get their meals in high chairs or hook-on seats when they can sit up all by themselves, usually at around six months. Earlier than this, even the most safely constructed high chair is a potential hazard because the baby could tip over or slide out.

In 1989, nearly 7700 children age four and younger were taken to hospitals because of injuries related to high chairs. Most of these children fell out of the chair, but some were injured by the chair itself: the chair collapsed while the child was in it or the child's fingers were pinched or crushed by the chair's tray. Preventing high chair falls is up to you: your child must be securely strapped into the chair each time you use it, but you cannot rely on the strap alone to keep a child safely seated. Remarkably young babies learn to wiggle, squirm, or slip out of their restraining straps. *Whenever a child is seated in a high chair, he must be monitored at all times*.

The makers of high chairs, like the makers of strollers and playpens, have agreed to voluntary safety standards set by the Juvenile Products Manufacturers Association. These standards include construction strong enough to hold up under 100 pounds, a safety belt with a crotch strap, no sharp edges or toxic material in the chair finish, locking devices on folding high chairs, the chair base made wider than the seat, and the chair legs slanting out for added stability. If a high chair complies with these provisions, it will carry a seal marked "certified" by the Juvenile Products Manufacturers Association: make sure the chair you purchase carries this seal.

Just as important as chair design is the way the chair is used. Always remember to:

• Be careful of your baby's fingers when sliding in or snapping on the tray. Get in the habit of saying, "Hands

Always monitor a child in a hook-on chair.

up!'' whenever you insert or remove the tray.
- Position the chair far enough from the table or counter so that the baby cannot push himself over with his feet. If possible, put the chair in a quiet corner of the kitchen so that older children or pets will not knock into it.
- Use the belt correctly each time you put your child in the chair. The tray is not designed as a restraining device and should not be used as a substitute for the belt.
- Store folding high chairs in places where babies (or toddlers) cannot get at them. A child can easily pull a collapsed chair over onto himself.

Hook-on chairs are baby-feeding chairs designed to hang on to the edge of your table. Two arms rest on top of the table and two curve under the table and are braced against it; what holds the chair securely in place is the child's weight. Parents like hook-on chairs because they're portable, light, can be used on most tables, and they bring the baby right into the action around the dining-room table instead of banishing him to the sidelines in a high chair. A baby can begin using a hook-on chair as soon as he can sit up by himself.

Hook-on chairs *are* handy to have, but you must be a little careful in buying and using them. Keep in mind that:

- A child in a hook-on chair will topple an unstable, light-weight, or rickety table. If the table wobbles, do not use one. Similarly do not use a hook-on chair with glass-top tables or tables with a pedestal base.
- An active playful baby can shake his hook-on chair right off the table and suffer a serious fall. To prevent this from happening, some manufacturers have installed safety clamps that lock the chair in place. These are effective, but not foolproof. Always monitor a child in a hook-on chair, check the chair's position, and dis-courage squirming or wiggling at the table.
- A chair, stool, or similar object must never be placed near a child in a hook-on chair. He could use it to push off with his feet and so work the chair loose from the table.
- Models equipped with a crotch bar and a seat belt are safest.
- A child over thirty pounds or even a very active lighter child should not be put in a hook-on chair. Once your baby begins to bounce, jiggle, or slide the chair along the table, it's time to stop using it.

You're set! Several hundred dollars poorer and many hours of shopping later, you are now thoroughly prepared to welcome your baby safely into your lives. Of course, once the baby *does* arrive, you're going to be using all this equipment and discovering all sorts of things you never dreamed of about how babies act and grow. A day with a baby is a hundred little acts of care and attention, and each little act brings up its own safety issues. For the basics of keeping your baby safe through the daily rou-tines of child care, read on . . .

2. Safety Through the Day

If you read Chapter 1 and followed its suggestions, your home is all set to receive your baby safely: you've got the right crib, the right car seat, a safely equipped nursery, appropriate clothing and toys. You know how to work all the buckles and straps, levers and catches, how to get your baby safely and comfortably in and out of each contraption. But mastery of equipment only takes you part of the way to safe infant care. Taking care of a baby involves a number of basic routines that you repeat each day and sometimes many times in the course of the day. For each one of these routines, there are certain safety measures all parents should be aware of. Again, common sense and instinct will be your natural guides in most situations, but there are some aspects of safe care that don't come as naturally as others and for which it's helpful to have the advice of experts and experienced parents.

As a baby grows rapidly in his first eighteen months, he rapidly adds new skills and abilities to his repertoire—sometimes more rapidly than parents are prepared for.

"Some of the developmental leaps have caught me by surprise," said one mother of a ten-month-old boy who fell out of his crib when she left him in it for a moment with the side down. She'd momentarily forgotten his new-found ability to stand. "When accidents have happened, it's because we haven't been ready for the next level of development." Each baby progresses at his own rate, but you should be prepared for wiggling and rolling by two months; grabbing objects (usually the smallest they can find) and instantly inserting them in the mouth by three months; creeping, humping, and squirming across a room by five months and crawling soon after; and standing, climbing, and maybe walking by ten months. Your baby may not keep pace with these milestones at the ages indicated (or may even be more advanced in some areas), but safe care indicates that you should try to be *prepared* for these activities at these ages. Remember: babies can master new skills with lightning speed. Your son can learn to climb a chair in a single day, to roll in a single afternoon. It's better to anticipate than regret.

Another issue parents face in the first eighteen months is how to balance restricting a child in the interest of safety with giving him the freedom he needs to explore and learn things for himself. "They need to learn what things do," said Julie, mother of a twenty-two-month-old girl and a four-month-old boy. "I don't just jerk things out of their hands and say, 'No!'" Rather, Julie takes the approach of letting them experiment with certain carefully chosen potential hazards—for example, the older child can play with her father's hammer and screwdrivers—while she watches them like a hawk

Mary, a mother of a toddler and a newborn who lives in Chapel Hill, North Carolina, takes a similar approach: "We give our toddler freedom, but we are right there—he is never out of our eyesight. When he's playing alone in his room, we leave the nursery monitor on so we can hear what he's doing. We never restricted his exploration and now we find that he does not take things that he isn't supposed to take. He listens.''

Often in finding the right balance between safety and exploration, we must make situation-by-situation assessments. There are times when parents find that a practical demonstration, for example, letting a child touch a hot (but not burning hot) radiator, teaches him faster and more effectively than a verbal instruction repeated a hundred times.

One of our goals as parents is to get our children to the point where they can make their own safe choices. With a baby just beginning to explore the new world around him, this goal seems an awfully long way off. But eventually you'll arrive there together, and the information covered in this chapter will help both of you proceed safely on your way.

Post in a clearly visible spot next to your phone these vital phone numbers and addresses:

Police:
Local Precinct:
Local Ambulance Service:
Hospital Emergency Room:
Private Doctor:
Poison Control Center:
Your Home Phone Number, Address, and Cross Street:

Handling

Many new parents, particularly new fathers, think babies are as fragile and delicate as spun glass. ''I held her like she was made of eggshells,'' said Pat of his newborn baby daughter. With time and practice we learn how amazingly sturdy they are: they don't break when the car goes over a bump or when the toddler from next door

(a)   **(b)**   **(c)**

(a) **Always support baby's head when picking her up or putting her down**...
(b) ...**cradle her head in the crook of your arm**...
(c) ...**or let her nestle her chin against your shoulder.**

comes over and pokes at their tummies. Babies are sturdier than they look, but they do have certain points of vulnerability that may not be immediately obvious. When handling a baby, keep in mind that:

- A baby's head needs to be supported whenever she is picked up or put down. Slip an open hand behind the back of her head and neck when you lift her and when you're holding her, cradle her head in the crook of your arm or let her chin nestle against your shoulder. Never let the baby's head flop or jerk back, as this will usually startle the baby into crying and could damage her neck.
- A baby has a soft spot, called a fontanel, at the top of her head. The soft spot, which is covered by a membrane, will be present until the four bones of the skull grow and fuse together during the first year. The soft spot's covering membrane is not really soft, in fact it's about as tough as canvas, so you don't have to worry about patting the baby's head, washing or combing her hair. But you should be careful that the fontanel is not poked, hit, or jabbed with a sharp instrument. If you notice that the fontanel is bulging out, the baby is prob-

ably sick and you should call a doctor; a fontanel that dips down is a sign of dehydration: rehydrate the baby by giving her diluted fruit juice or water.

• A baby should never be lifted by or held with all of her weight suspended from her hands, elbows, or arms. This strains young ligaments and it could dislocate her shoulders. Once your baby can hold her head up herself, you'll find the best way to lift her is to slip your hands under her armpits with your open hands supporting her around the chest and back.

Feeding

As long as your baby is eating only breast milk or formula, your major safety consideration about feeding is *hygiene*. The person feeding the baby, whether from the breast or bottle, should wash her or his hands before the feeding and a nursing mother should make sure her nipples are clean and free of infection. It's a good idea to let nipples dry in the air after each feeding and to wash away dried milk at least twice a day (avoid soap, since it may wash away skin oils that help keep the nipples from cracking).

One advantage of breast milk is that it's ready to drink, perfectly warmed, and needs no refrigeration (expressed breast milk should be refrigerated or frozen). With formula, you must take care in the way you prepare it, store it, and clean the equipment you use. The primary concern here is bacteria that grow quickly in the formula and in the bottles and nipples that the formula passes through. When using formula, follow these hygiene tips:

• When mixing up a batch of formula, follow the instructions on the can closely. Be sure to wipe clean the tops of cans.
• Work in a clean area with a clean can opener, tongs etc.

To be extra safe, some parents sterilize all the equipment in boiling water.

- Bottles should be clean and dry. Most pediatricians feel that scrubbing out bottles and nipples in hot soapy water with a bottle and a nipple brush or running them through the dishwasher is enough. However, some parents prefer to sterilize bottles and nipples either by immersing them in boiling water or in a bottle sterilizer made expressly for this purpose.
- Use a batch of formula within 48 hours of mixing it or opening a premixed can. Throw out what you haven't used by this time and mix a new batch.
- Discard half-drunk bottles after they have sat out for one hour. If you return them promptly to the refrigerator, you may keep them for four hours.
- Never mix the leftover contents of a bottle with a fresh bottle.
- Rinse out bottles promptly after the baby has drunk the formula. Bacteria breed in standing mild and dried crusted milk is much harder to clean off than fresh milk.

When bottle-feeding a baby, *never prop the baby up on her back or side with the bottle*. A baby left unattended with a bottle is at serious risk of choking and could have difficulty breathing.

Starting Solids

Once your baby begins eating solid foods (i.e., vegetables, fruits, meats, and starches that have been strained, mashed, pureed, etc.) at anytime from four to seven months (ask the pediatrician when to begin), you have to be much more careful about choking and allergic reactions.

Infant Allergies

Foods to which babies are most commonly allergic are:

- cow's milk
- egg whites
- wheat
- corn
- pork
- fish
- rhubarb
- shellfish
- onions
- citrus fruits (along with tomatoes and pineapple)
- chocolate
- peanut butter
- nuts
- berries

Signs of allergic reactions to foods include:

- wheezing
- vomiting
- rash
- sore bottom
- diarrhea
- constipation

If your baby shows any one of these signs after eating a new food, discontinue that food at once and let the doctor know. To be safe, start the baby on one new food at a time and give him only a small amount of it. Wait three to five days to see how he's taking it before giving more or before starting on a new food. When you're in the process of testing the baby on new foods, stay away from stews, soups, and multi-grain cereals since the multitude of ingredients in these dishes makes it impossible for you to identify exactly which food is causing an allergy.

As a matter of general hygiene, make it a practice never to feed the baby directly from the baby-food jar (if you plan to reuse it) and never to serve prepared foods that you're planning to save (for example, applesauce, cooked beans) with a utensil that has been in someone's mouth. If you've been storing something in your refrigerator for a while, check it for freshness before serving it to your child.

Foods that Babies Should Never Be Given

The reason all of these foods are forbidden is that they can easily lodge in a baby's throat and block off the windpipe, causing the baby to suffocate.

• nuts, especially peanuts
• chunky peanut butter
• whole grapes
• fruits with seeds or pits or thick skins
• whole-grain breads with very big pieces of grain
• hard candy
• popcorn
• raw carrots or small slices of raw vegetables
• whole hot dogs

You can reduce the risk of choking on grapes or hot dogs by cutting them up: slice grapes in half or quarters and remove the seeds; peel the hot dog, slice it lengthwise in half, and then cut each half into bite-size pieces.

For emergency treatment for choking, see p. 000 In Case of Emergency.

Babies under age one should also never be given honey because of the high risk of infant botulism. Once they pass their first birthday, honey ceases to be a problem.

Even after they get their teeth, many babies have trouble chewing and swallowing meat. "My kids have trouble with chicken and beef," said Sandy, mother of two boys ages four-and-a-half and fifteen months. "They chew them until they're wadded up like gum, then they gag and spit it out." You can help them out by putting cooked meats through a food processor, blender, or meat grinder or by making sure that they only take a small amount in their mouths at a time and that they have swallowed what they've taken before you give them more.

Safe Meals

Janet, the mother of an eleven-month-old girl and a four-year-old boy, said her advice about safety at meal times was "to watch them every minute. What you think might be harmless could easily make them gag or choke. There are solids they can't break up easily or they might have too much in their mouths. So watch them as they eat."

For safe use of high chairs, see Chapter 1, p. 000. Remember that it is essential to use the strap whenever a child sits in the high chair. Kathryn, the mother of four in Virginia Beach, Virginia, reports that when her younger boy was eleven months old, "I took the tray off the high chair and he dived out even though I was standing right there. He landed right on his head. I learned the hard way always to use the belt."

Keep in mind, however, that a high chair crotch strap will restrain a child, but is not a guarantee of safety. I always strapped our daughter in and I assumed the straps would keep her in place, until the day I went down the hall to get a washcloth and came back to find her standing up in the chair. One mother reported that her son had wriggled free of his straps and managed to stand up on the high chair tray in the time it took her to cross the kitchen. If you can't be with your baby the entire time she's in the high chair, take her down out of the chair or get someone else to mind her.

Kristin, the mother of a toddler boy and an eight-month-old girl, said that she will not give her children food to eat unless they are sitting and that she avoids taking along in the car any foods that might choke them, for example, a grape that could lodge in the throat when the car goes over a bump.

Dressing and Changing

Consumer Products Safety Commission statistics indicate that each year 1400 babies sustain injuries in accidents related to improper use of changing tables—the vast majority being falls. One mother of two described a close call with her eleven-month-old son: "He was strapped to the changing table, but he flipped off when I turned around for a second and I found him hanging head down. When you're changing the baby—whether on a changing table or bed—you can't run into the next room just to answer the phone or doorbell. Pick him up and take him with you: it's easier all around and safer, too." And, I might add, that while the baby is on the changing table, it's a good idea to maintain constant hand contact with him even if he's strapped.

Another mother said that once her daughter became

very active and squirmy at around nine months, she started dressing her in the crib with the side down instead of on the changing table. This is fine so long as you remember to raise the side of the crib if you have to leave the room. Ginny, the mother of a seven-month-old boy, said she forgot to do this once when her son was just learning to stand. She had assumed that he would stay put, but that was the moment he made the breakthrough to pulling himself up unassisted and went toppling out of the crib (luckily nothing serious happened). Kristin avoided any dangers from falling by changing her two children on the floor.

Wherever you're changing your baby's diapers, make sure that she can't grab any of the ointments, pins, premoistened wipes, and other potentially hazardous paraphernalia. Kristin said her son grabbed a diaper pin when she had turned her head for a second: he was so young, she assumed he couldn't pick up objects yet. Most baby care authorities today discourage the use of baby powder or corn starch because there is no evidence whatever that they prevent or cure diaper rash. If you do use powder of any sort, be sure that you don't shake it out of the container in clouds that the baby could inhale. Pour a small amount in your hand and then pat on the baby's bottom. Don't use zinc stearate powders in any form: these have been proven to be irritating to babies' lungs. Be particularly careful where and how you store powder containers. Infants have died by getting hold of an open powder container, raising it to their mouths, and sucking in. If you have a climbing toddler in the house, keep powders out of his range—or better yet, get rid of them. Pediatricians also discourage parents from using baby oils and researchers have issued warnings against ointments containing iodochlorhydroxyquin. A far better cure for diaper rash than any ointment or powder is to expose the baby's bottom to the air for as long as convenience and climate permit. Use mild soaps in the baby's bath and keep the diaper area dry by changing diapers frequently. In the case of serious and persistent diaper rash, consult your pediatrician.

Dealing With Cloth Diapers

If you're using cloth diapers, you must sterilize them in a special soaking solution before washing them (or exchanging them for a fresh batch provided by the diaper service). Cloth diapers that have not been properly sterilized, washed, and dried can irritate a baby's skin, bring on diaper rash, and breed bacteria that cause infection. As soon as you remove the diaper from the baby, you should rinse it if it's only wet or scrape or shake the stool into the toilet. Then rinse it in the sink or toilet to dissolve away the stain. Wring diapers dry and then drop them in the sterilizing pail: this is a covered pail that holds sterilizing solution (a mixture of either water and soaking bleach or water and commercially sold diaper sterilizer). After soaking diapers for at least six hours, drain them in the sink (or by spinning them in the washing machine *before* washing), then wash in the machine using hot water and mild soap. Rinse the diapers at least twice and dry them thoroughly.

The advantage of a diaper service is that all you have to do is rinse the diapers and store them in the sterilizing pail (some services offer chemically treated diapers that only need to be stored in plastic-lined hampers after use). The diaper service does the washing and drying.

Bathing

The one cardinal rule of bathing a baby safely is: *Never leave the baby alone in the bath, even for an instant.* A child can drown in less than two inches of water and can damage herself seriously in the time it takes you to answer the phone or go hunt for a towel. Even bathtubs equipped with nonslip stickers are hazardous for young, unsupervised children, and it doesn't take much imagination to realize how perilous the combination of a slippery bathtub, water, and hard porcelain can be. When you're bathing an infant who can't reliably sit up by herself, you not only must stay with her every second, but keep a constant grip on her in the tub. Support her back with one hand and wash her with the other.

Do not give a newborn a tub bath until the umbilical-cord scab has dried and fallen off and the navel is entirely healed. Instead, give the newborn a sponge bath, working down from face to feet. Use dampened and squeezed out sterile cotton balls to clean the face—take a fresh cotton ball for each eye. If the boy has been circumcised, don't bathe him until his penis is healed. If the boy has not been circumcised, do not attempt to retract the foreskin for cleaning the penis. Just wash the outside of the penis. Later on when the foreskin loosens up, it will retract easily (usually at around four years of age) and then you can wash under it. Eventually you'll be able to teach a boy to retract the foreskin and wash by himself. Similarly only wash the outside of a girl's vagina—never open the labia to clean inside. Girls should be wiped from front to back so that you won't spread fecal bacteria from the anus to the vagina.

Here are a few more tips gathered from parents for safety in the bath:

- During early infancy, use special infant bathtubs in which the baby can recline without needing your support.
- Only fill the bath with a few inches of water.
- A pad, towel, or large sponge can be placed under the baby in the bath to prevent slipping.

- Only use the mildest, non-perfumed soap and non-sting baby shampoo.
- Wash the baby's face first, then body and genitals.
- There is no need to bathe a young baby daily (unless he loves his bath).
- A baby should never be allowed to stand or play too wildly in the bath.
- Do not let toddlers climb in or out of the bath by themselves.

Playing

Babies love to play and even to roughhouse at a surprisingly young age. Don't be timid about hugging, patting, tickling, and rolling around with your baby. But do take some care that roughhousing is not *too* rough. In particular, when playing with an infant, you should never:

- Lift or swing the baby by the arms or hands.
- Toss the baby in the air (this could damage the neck).
- Let the baby's head flop back abruptly on his neck.
- Bang the baby's soft spot (see above).

Otherwise, let your baby's reactions be your guide in play. If he's enjoying himself, he'll let you know; just as he won't leave you in any doubt when he's miserable.

Outings

Babies love to go out for walks, shopping trips, visits, or just out in the park or yard for quiet snoozes under a tree. The right equipment—stroller, carriage, front carrier, backpack—will make these outings easier for you and safer for your baby (for a discussion of safe equipment for outings, see Chapter 1, p. 000). But you still have to take some care to guard your baby from the elements and from the wrong contact with strangers.

Use common sense and moderation when taking out newborns and infants. Avoid prolonged exposure to extreme heat or cold. Newborn babies should not go outside when it's colder than 40 degrees. If you must take them out (for example, to the doctor) dress them warmly, make sure their heads, ears, hands, and feet are well-covered, heat the inside of the car before taking the baby outside or try to have a taxi waiting at the door so you don't have to stand in the cold. Remember, babies lose body heat quickly, particularly through the head, so on cold days always put a warm, securely fitting hat on them and wrap them in a snowsuit or down-filled infant sack.

When the weather is very hot and sunny, you must take care to protect the baby from sunburn, overheating, and dehydration. Do not overdress babies on hot days (check the back of the baby's neck for sweat) but make certain he is well covered in light clothing to protect his skin from the sun. An infant can get a serious sunburn in fifteen minutes! Best is to keep the baby in the shade (thus if you go to the beach bring a big umbrella) and to keep his head covered with a light cap or sunbonnet. If the baby is going to be exposed to the sun for any period of time (for example, in a parking lot or out walking) it's especially important to cover him and to apply sunblock to exposed skin every three hours. For a very fair-skinned baby, apply the sunblock fifteen or twenty minutes before he will be out in the sun so it has a chance to soak in. Babies with very sensitive skin will break out in a rash from some brands of sunblock: look for a product designed specifically for babies. When washing your baby's face at the end of the day, take care to keep the sunblock from getting in his eyes.

Adults need to replenish their body fluids on very hot days and so do babies. Offer water often.

Use common sense when exposing your baby to other people, not only strangers but also friends and family. Hordes of well-wishers traipsing through your house to take a peek at the new arrival will exhaust both of you and increase the risk of the baby getting some infection. A baby is even more likely to pick up a cold in a crowded bus, subway, or store during the fall and winter months when so many infections are going around. If you don't want strangers touching, patting, or stroking your baby, say so. Some parents prefer friends and relatives to wash their hands before picking up their newborn.

A generation ago, it was all but unheard of for babies to be snatched from their parents in public places, but today's headlines have made everyone aware that this is now a real and serious concern. "We haven't had any trouble with it in this area," said Janet, a mother of two from rural New Hampshire, "but it's still a real concern. Whenever I go out, my baby daughter is buckled into her backpack and for my toddler son I use a hand-holder strapped to my wrist. That way he has some freedom if he doesn't want to hold my hand, but I feel confident because I have him where I want him." Julie, also the mother of a toddler and an infant, says she doesn't take her kids out to large shopping areas or malls (they live on a farm in Lonetree, Iowa) unless her husband is along to help mind them. Stephanie, the mother of a fourteen-month-old in Renton, Washington, said she never leaves her daughter alone in the car, "Even if it's in front of a glass window three feet away where I can see her. I just won't take the risk." Betsy described how frightened she felt when a strange woman asked to hold her baby in a department store. She was too embarrassed to refuse, but she positioned herself between the woman and the exit, poised to give chase. Though nothing happened, she said she wouldn't put herself in this situation again. The moral of the story is: don't let yourself be embarrassed into doing something you consider unwise or unsafe for your baby.

Your baby cannot be watched too carefully or kept too close in public. When taking your children into a public place:

- Never leave them alone *even for a minute*.
- Never leave children by themselves in the car *even if it's locked* (children have died by releasing the hand brake and by playing with the car cigarette lighter).
- Try to maintain hand contact with the stroller or shopping cart in which your baby is riding.
- Remember that you won't be able to monitor a baby in a backpack—so avoid this type of carrier in very crowded places or in stores where the baby could grab merchandise.
- Do not let strangers hold or carry your baby. If the person seems trustworthy and friendly, *you* pick up the baby and let him or her have a good look.

Protecting a baby from snatching doesn't mean going through life with total paranoia and suspicion. Rather, it's a matter of avoiding unnecessary risks and maintaining a little extra vigilance. In time, these precautions like so many others will become second nature.

Siblings

We all want our children to love each other, and usually they do—eventually—but along the way there can be some rough moments. Toddlers and preschoolers are impulsive and strong and still too young to control some of their more hostile emotions. Babies have been hurt and even killed by older siblings. Therefore it is imperative to protect babies from the aggression and roughness of older siblings, particularly in the early months. Keep young babies out of the paths of playing toddlers and, if you have seen cause for worry, never leave the baby alone in the room with an aggressive older child. A toddler can easily climb into a baby's carriage, playpen, and even crib, or pull an infant seat off a counter. Be especially careful never to leave the baby alone with a toddler when there is water in a pool, tub, or even a large basin.

Though most older siblings resent a new arrival, they are almost always curious about the baby as well, and you can use this curiosity to interest them in explanations about safety with babies. Tell them about the baby's soft spot (see above) and explain why the baby must never be dropped, bitten, or stepped on. Art, a father from Provo, Utah of an active toddler and seven-month-old twins (all three are boys), said that he and his wife try to make the toddler more aware of his actions around the babies by discussion rather than punishment: "If he steps on the twins accidentally, we explain to him what he's done. We try to slow him down, even at the risk of making him less spontaneous around the babies." Eventually the babies will grow big enough to fend for themselves (at least some of the time).

You must be especially careful that babies cannot get at unsafe toys of older siblings. In a large and active family this may be nearly impossible and you may have to confiscate unsafe toys until the baby grows up. Kathryn, the mother of a six-year-old, a three-year-old, a two-year-old, and a one-year-old, had to take away all the Legos with small pieces from the older kids and replace them with Duplo blocks that were too large for her baby to swallow. Her six-year-old is old enough to put his things away in closets or up on high shelves, but the three-year-old tends to throw things into the baby's playpen. Kathryn emphasizes the importance of watching them every minute. She also has made the situation a bit easier on herself by teaching the older children certain safety rules—for example, always to close the toilet lid. This makes them more aware of safety and keeps down the amount of mischief the baby can get into.

Just as babies can get into trouble with a toddler's toys, so toddlers can hurt themselves when playing unsupervised with equipment meant for the baby. Our two-and-a-half-year-old daughter climbed into and tipped over the twins' carriage twice the day we brought them home from the hospital (luckily, neither baby was in it); she tried to eat their Vaseline; and showed great interest in their diaper pins. While we were busy protecting the babies from their active older sister, we had neglected all the new hazards to our toddler we had introduced with the baby equipment. It seemed odd to childproof baby equipment, but it was necessary.

Pets

Pets are unpredictable around small children and children are unpredictable around pets. You hear stories of fierce hunting dogs lying quietly while babies pull their tails and crawl all over them—and you also hear about kindly, devoted old house dogs growling and snapping at little ones. Pets get jealous, they misinterpret curious babies' enthusiasm for aggression, they become frightened when children corner them; babies are often tireless pet chasers as soon as they're mobile and once they're up and walking, they may provoke an animal by hitting, twisting its ears, or yanking its tail.

For these reasons, you should make it a general rule *never to leave a child under the age of six unsupervised with a pet*.

If your pet predates your baby, make a special effort to introduce the baby to the pet gradually. Some advise bringing home a diaper or an undershirt from the hospital for the dog to sniff before the baby arrives. Don't neglect the pet altogether in the first weeks your baby is home. A few extra treats may keep jealousy at bay. Be careful of cats jumping into the baby's carriage and clawing or even licking the baby with their coarse tongues.

As your baby enters each new stage of development (from immobile to crawling, crawling to walking) you may have to exercise special vigilance around the pets for a while. As far as the animal is concerned, a crawling baby is an entirely different creature than a babe in arms and the pet may treat the baby as a stranger for a time. Our dogs pretty much ignored our older daughter at first, but once she learned to crawl, one of them began growling at her every time she headed his way. It became necessary to discipline the dog and to get between him and the baby when she came at him full tilt. Once she could walk, the animals calmed down a lot. Now, as a toddler, she's the aggressor and the dogs hide behind us for protection.

Teach your baby from the very start to be gentle with pets and model the behavior you want her to have. If she sees you yelling at and whacking the dog all the time, she will imitate you as soon as she's able.

A child who has grown up with gentle, loving pets needs to be taught that all animals are not as friendly as her own. "My daughter has gotten used to our house dog, and now she tries to feed the farm cats," said a mother of two who lives on a farm in Iowa. "These are outdoor cats and once one of them clamped down on her hand. Luckily it didn't break the skin. I've tried to teach her to stay away from the cats and not to hit them. If she thinks it's okay to hit the cats, she may try the same thing on her baby brother when he pulls her hair."

The general rule for strange animals is: look but do not touch.

Baby-sitters

Much as we love our babies, we can't always and don't always want to be with them. When we're away, we want to make sure the baby-sitters we choose are competent, careful, and aware of safety matters. Too many parents make the mistake of *assuming* that the baby-sitter will know what to do in every circumstance. This is a particular problem with teenagers and baby-sitters without much experience with young children. Even the brightest, most responsible sixteen-year-old may not realize that a four-month-old baby can flip off the changing table in the wink of an eye or pick up a penny and pop it in his mouth. So, when you're using a baby-sitter for the first time, take the time to go over *every* aspect of the routine, explaining how you do things, where things are, what your baby can do in terms of climbing, pulling down objects, potential fighting between siblings, etc. You can't be too specific. Review such subjects as stair safety, forbidden foods, the dangers of climbing and falling, allergies your child has, safety with pets. Stephanie, who uses two or three different baby-sitters for her fourteen-month-old daughter, says she has a "baby-sitter memo board in the kitchen on which I list where the fire extinguisher is, where to find the first aid kit, and where I post emergency phone numbers (for a list of vital emergency numbers to post, see above). I always remind the sitters to put the railing up on the baby's crib and to make sure the stairwell gate is in place."

Remind yourself that aspects of baby care that are second nature to you may be entirely unknown to someone who doesn't have children or hasn't been around children in some time (even your own parents may not have taken care of a baby since you were one yourself: they may need a refresher course).

Other tips for choosing and instructing baby-sitters:

- Try to find a baby-sitter who has experience and is a known quantity (i.e., one who has worked for friends or family members or is known to friends or church or synagogue members).
- If you don't know the baby-sitter personally, ask for references and check them out before hiring the person.

- Never hire a baby-sitter younger than twelve-years-old.
- When using a baby-sitter for the first time, have the person come a few hours early so you can acquaint him or her with the basics of care and safety and so your baby can get used to him or her.
- Post all emergency numbers (fire, police, doctor, ambulance) next to the phone and show the baby-sitter where they are.
- Give the baby-sitter the phone number and address of where you will be and the approximate time of your stay.
- Make sure the baby-sitter knows *your* home address and cross street so he or she can direct police or ambulance there in case of emergency.

(For more on hiring a reliable care giver or finding safe day care, see Chapter 7.)

Visiting

When you take your baby visiting, remember that a strange house presents new hazards, often hazards that your hosts are not even aware of. If you are going to be staying with friends or relatives for any length of time, it might be wise to help them baby proof their homes (see the following chapter) or to remove obvious hazards when you arrive. Bring a child safety gate so you can block off unsafe areas of the house.

One hazard that many of us neglect while visiting (or while receiving visitors in our homes) is a woman's handbag. Usually these are full of cosmetics, pills, coins, and other potentially dangerous objects, and when they're lying on the floor or draped across a chair, they offer an irresistible temptation to curious little ones. Make sure pocketbooks are safely stored in closed closets or out of reach on shelves.

Starting to Talk About Safety

"The sooner you start, the sooner they learn" was the advice of a mother of two for when to begin talking with young children about safety matters.

"When you have a baby, you gain an immediate respect for him as a person," another mother put it, "so it makes perfect sense right from the start to explain things to him as you would to anyone."

"You can't start all of a sudden out of the blue," said a mother of four, "because it may be too late. I started as soon as they started moving."

"I started telling our older boy [now two] *no* when he was really young—about six months," said one father of three. "We haven't had any major problems because we started so young. You cannot eliminate their curiosity, but if you keep repeating *no*, they will eventually respond."

Long before he can talk, your baby can understand what you say, and before he can understand words, he can understand tone of voice. Better ultimately than any amount of safe equipment or special vigilance on our part is to make our children realize on their own the potential dangers around them—and this process can begin in a calm, low-key way in the earliest months. "We discuss safety matters a little at a time," said Janet. "We don't want to dump it all at once. So with my eleven-month-old we're teaching her about hot. With the four-year-old we're going through strangers and crossing the street safely." Stephanie also started discussing safety early with her daughter, and now the fourteen-month-old sometimes initiates such conversations: "She will point to the stove and pull away, then she looks at me until I say 'hot'! She's good about listening so long as I change my tone of voice and sound like I really mean it."

Usually the way parents begin discussing safety matters with their babies is to designate certain *nos* and certain hard-and-fast rules around the house. For example, in Ginny's apartment, going into the fireplace is a *no*, climbing on the dining-room table is a *no*, pulling cords on the iron, hair dryer, and other electrical appliances is a *no*, reaching up to the stove is an *absolute no*, climbing near windows is a *no*, playing on or under the glass table is a *no*. As soon as he was mobile, Ginny's son was taught that these things were off-limits to him and now, even though he is a headstrong toddler, he obeys.

Other common household *no*s include:

- playing in the toilet
- standing up in the bath
- standing or rocking in the high chair or the booster seat
- pulling or chewing on electrical cords
- playing in the laundry room, the sewing room, the workshop
- handling knives and scissors
- opening screens or outside doors
- playing with ashtrays or cigarettes
- turning on water faucets (especially hot)
- going outside alone and unannounced
- playing near wood-burning stoves
- playing in the garbage
- teasing pets

You can safeguard against some of these things by baby proofing (see the following chapter), but it still makes sense to begin teaching your baby what is dangerous and why. "We have taught him the word *dangerous* and he adheres," said Mary of her toddler. "Whenever I open the stove I say, 'It's hot,' and now he has learned to back away and say, 'Mommy—*hot!*'" Another mother emphasized the importance of repetition. She once found her newly walking son playing in the toilet water and she explained to him that toilet water is not for drinking or playing with. Every time he reached for the toilet, she would repeat this and then lower the top of the toilet seat. Now the child has learned the lesson so well that he lowers the toilet seat by himself if his parents have left it up.

Mary had some more good advice about making sure that little ones are *really* listening when we're explaining safety rules to them. In order to get her son's attention, she'll ask, "Do you have your listening ears on?" It makes safety instruction into something of a game and it also signals that she really wants him to concentrate on what she's saying.

Janet also had a good tip for how to make young children pay attention: "When I say *no* to my eleven-month-old, I look at her eye-to-eye. I tell her what she's doing is wrong and then I pick her up and take her away. If you really want them to get the idea, it's important not to leave them where they're getting in trouble. Back up your words with actions."

Talking about safety and establishing firm household rules is important, but you don't want to go overboard, especially with a young child. "I hate saying *no* all the time," one mother commented. "The attitude I take is that if I'm around and watching him, I give him pretty much free rein." Another mother explained, "We haven't gone through the house saying, 'You can't do this, you can't do that.' We feel this would add temptation." Both of these parents acknowledge that the price of giving their children more freedom is that they have to be extra vigilant (this may not be possible with more than one child). These mothers have also found that although their children get into more things more quickly, as they get older they also listen and obey more readily.

It's a good idea to try to make safety discussions a part of everyday life, discussing rules before a confrontation gets going, repeating them firmly but without anger, drawing a safety moral from the books you read to our children, and patiently explaining (and re-explaining) *why* something is unsafe. This last point is especially important as babies grow into toddlerhood. As the child's grasp of cause and effect increases, she can really comprehend the *reason* things are unsafe: we don't touch the stove because it's hot; we don't pull the cat's tail because he scratches, etc. Thus explaining becomes a far more effective way of enforcing safe behavior than merely dictating *don't touch, don't pull*, etc. By explaining the whys and hows to your child, you will also make safety a part of the wonderful process by which she learns about the world.

3. All About Baby Proofing

For better or for worse, worrying is part of the job description of parents. We worry about how our children grow, how they sleep, how they will cope with change; we worry about their physical, mental, and social developments; we worry about their eating and excreting habits; we worry in a minutely specific, moment-by-moment way about their present and in a vague, cosmic, dreamlike way about their future. And, of course, we worry about their safety. Injuries from electrical outlets or fireplaces; choking; burns; drowning; falling down stairs; cuts from knives or breakable objects; injuries from falls; poisoning—these are the safety worries that head the lists of the parents I interviewed.

As any experienced worrier can tell you, the best way to quell worries is to have some control over the things we worry about. Controlling a child's future or her rate of physical development is pretty much out of our hands— but controlling her safety, at least to some extent, is within our reach. One of the most important and one of the most practical ways of exercising this safe control is through baby proofing. Baby proofing is not a foolproof guarantee of safety, and it certainly is no substitute for loving, attentive care, but it can and does make a world of difference. A difference, first of all, for our children who can play and grow without being subjected to unnecessary hazards and without being reprimanded at every turn; and a difference for us in not only allaying many of our safety worries, but in freeing up the way we monitor our children. When we baby proof our homes, we don't have to stand over our children every second; we can let them explore (within earshot) with the assurance that they won't get into danger, and we'll avoid conflicts down the road in the toddler years when little ones test our wills and patience by trying to get at forbidden objects.

"I don't have to baby proof—I'll take the time to teach my little girl about household dangers" is a tack that many parents take. It's an approach that simply does not work. Yes, our children can learn lots of things very quickly; but no, they cannot be trusted to obey in their infancy and toddler years. Many of us are astonished to see babies not even a year old hold up their hands when they approach a forbidden cabinet and declare "No!" with a firm head shake. But there comes a time for almost all children when the "No!" becomes too tempting to resist. We're in the bathroom, on the phone, changing the newborn's diaper—and that's the moment our sixteen-month-old explorer chooses to see for himself. One father told a very sad story about a mother he knew who boasted that her daughter was so obedient and well trained that no baby proofing was necessary: she learned how wrong she was when the little girl got under the sink and began to experiment with the scouring powders. There are lots of similar stories.

Enough preaching. Granted, we've all accepted the need for baby proofing. The first question is: When do we do it? The answer is: baby proof before your baby can creep or crawl (around six months), update once he can climb and walk (ten months to one year), and update periodically as he grows and becomes stronger, bigger, and more inventive.

The next question is: How do we do it? The guiding principle of baby proofing a house, whether for an infant or a toddler, is: *Be methodical*. Go through the entire house. Get down on your hands and knees and take a look at the world from your child's perspective. You may feel a bit foolish, but it's amazing how many things you'll discover that you might have overlooked from five or six feet up (for example, the edges and undersides of low tables; splinters from wood floors; electrical outlets hidden behind chair legs). Look under chests or drawers and radiators (one father found broken glass heaped up in a place the broom didn't reach but his baby probably would have), behind sofas, between bookcases and walls, in out of the way corners. Babies love to squeeze into tiny spaces and they're ingenious at finding tiny objects—so be more thorough and more ingenious than they are. One father of a two-year-old boy and twin seven-month-old babies says he has to check through the house for dangerous small objects nearly every day. "You always have to think twice about what might be down on their level," he commented.

This chapter covers the basics of baby proofing for the standard home, and it will certainly get you started. But undoubtedly there will be special features of your own home not covered here. After you follow the suggestions here, go through your house *again* from a baby's perspective and take care of anything else that may have been left out. To assist you in your baby-proofing efforts, the chapter includes a checklist of potential hazards that may be present in any room in your house and a checklist of dangerous household objects and substances, including plants. The chapter also covers baby proofing the house room by room, and then moves outside the house to the garage, yard, and pool.

Baby proofing doesn't cost a lot and it doesn't take a

lot of time; but what time and money it takes are well spent. There is no question that it pays off.

Home-Accident Statistics

These statistics on home accidents are not meant to frighten you. Rather, their purpose is to alert you to the major dangers to young children present in our homes and to guide you accordingly in your baby proofing efforts.

According to statistics compiled by the National Safety Council, some 2,200 children from birth to age four died during 1988 in accidents suffered at home. The two biggest killers were fire and water: 800 children in this age-group died in fires or by injuries caused by fires such as asphyxiation, falls, falling objects; 350 children in this age-group died in drowning accidents, including accidents in swimming pools and bathtubs. Suffocation by smothering in bedclothes, plastic bags, or cave-ins accounted for 220 deaths of children in this group, and suffocation by ingesting or inhaling objects or food killed another 250 children. Home poisonings claimed 100 children in the birth to four age-group and falls claimed another 110.

Many of these deaths, especially those caused by poisoning, suffocation, falls, and drowning, could have been prevented by adequate child proofing.

Baby Proofing Checklist

Any room in any house or apartment could have these hazards. Here's what to do about them:

Electrical Outlets:

Potential injury: Could cause a fatal shock if a child inserts a metal object.

Cover all unused outlets with plastic covers.

To baby proof: Cover all unused outlets with plastic cover (available in hardware stores). Make sure the brand you buy is not impossible for *you* to remove and replace.

Electrical Appliances:

Potential injury: Burns to fingers, mouth, or face. Child will suffer electrical shock if he touches a plugged-in appliance with wet hands or with his mouth.

To baby proof: Keep all electrical appliances including the toaster, coffee pot, hair dryer, curling iron, blender out of your baby's reach. Never leave a child alone in a room while an appliance is plugged in. Wrap the cord around the appliance when not in use and put it away. Make sure all accessible lamps have light bulbs securely screwed into all sockets.

Electrical cords, telephone cords, wires, extension cords:

Potential injury: Electrical burn on the mouth if a child chews through the cord. Abrasion or burn to the head or the body from pulling the appliance down by the cord. Possible strangulation on the cord.

To baby proof: Run cords and wires under carpets; tape or nail them along the edge of baseboards; wrap excess cord around the base of the appliance so a child cannot tug on them; always unplug appliances (toaster, hair dryer, curling iron, coffee pot) and the extension cord when not in use, wrap the cord around the appliance, bind up the extension cord, and put it out of reach. Minimize your use of extension cords, and discard old, frayed, or faulty cords.

Cords on Curtains, Blinds, Window Shades:

Potential injury: Strangulation if the baby wraps the cord around her neck.

To baby proof: Get the excess cord out of the baby's reach either by gathering it up and securing it in a tight bundle (use a plastic tie or rubber band), hanging the cord high on the wall or window frame (adhesive teacup hooks are useful for this), or by looping the cord over some other piece of hardware.

Furniture with Sharp Edges:

Potential injury: Cuts and bruises from falls or by walking or running into the piece of furniture.

To baby proof: Cover edges with cushioned, adhesive corner covers (look in baby-furniture stores or catalogues).

Windows:

Potential injury: Severe injury from falls, breaking glass.

To baby proof: Cover accessible windows with child-safety screens similar to a baby gate—see below (standard window screens are *not* strong enough to keep a child from pushing or kicking through). Or purchase window locks that will prevent a child from opening the window.

Avoid placing furniture under windows to minimize the possibility of climbing.

Glass Furniture, Objects:

Potential injury: Cuts from breaking the furniture (glass coffee table, for example) or object.

To baby proof: Remove breakables. Make all your glass furniture off-limits to your child. If that doesn't work, remove the furniture or lock it away in another room.

Unstable Furniture (Wobbly Bookshelves or Tables, Hutch Resting on Top of Another Piece):

Potential injury: Broken bones, concussion from a child pulling the piece of furniture over on top of herself.

To baby proof: Bolt the hutch, bookshelf, wall unit, or any tall piece of furniture to the wall. Reinforce wobbly tables or, if that is impossible, remove the unsafe pieces.

Fireplaces, Wood-Burning Stoves, Radiators, Space Heaters:

Potential injury: Burns, poisoning, or damage to lungs from ingesting soot, fuel, or lighter fluid; cuts or eye injury from sharp andirons or other fireplace tools; burning down the house from knocking over the heater or throwing an inflammable object on it.

To baby proof: Always cover the fireplace with a child-proof screen and if possible block off the wood stove or radiator with a gate or with other furniture. Never place a space heater (or steam vaporizer) within a child's reach or near enough his crib for him to throw his covers onto it. If the fireplace is not in use, remove the andirons and tools (a child should *not* be allowed to explore an unused fireplace since soot is a hazard if inhaled). Teach your baby that the fireplace and the stove are *no*s. Even with all these precautions, *if a fireplace or stove is lit, or if a space heater or steam vaporizer is in use, never leave a child alone in the room.*

Scatter Rugs:

Potential injury: Scrapes and bruises from falls.
To baby proof: Remove rugs until the baby is steadier on her feet.

Stairs and Gates

The conventional baby proofing wisdom on how to take care of stairs in the home is to block them off with gates. There is no doubt that gates are necessary to protect the baby from toppling down a flight of steps—but safest of all is to use gates *in conjunction with* teaching the baby how to navigate stairs safely. That way, if you or a houseguest ever leave the gate open accidentally (or if an older child plays with it and leaves it open), your baby will have an added measure of safety should he decide to explore the stairs.

The first stairs lesson your baby should learn is *never* to go on the stairs without you. Teach him that stairs are potentially dangerous and explain why. When your baby has reached the crawling and climbing stage, you can begin to show him the safe way to go up and down stairs. Going up is usually no problem for curious climbers; however make sure you remind the baby not to try to stand up on the stairs, but to crawl up on his hands and knees. Then teach the baby to go down the stairs on his tummy by sliding feet from one step down to the next. We had good success with our daughter by demonstrating the technique ourselves, by gently moving her arms and legs through the positions, and by demonstrating again using a large doll. One mother lured her baby down the steps by placing a favorite toy at the bottom. Repetition is the key to success. Make it a kind of serious game (no horseplay on stairs) and keep at it. You may have to repeat the lesson for months until the child catches on. Eventually he will, and in the process he'll learn that stairs are a serious matter that require extra precaution.

Finally make sure you always keep the stairs clear. Never use them for temporary storage. Even a single piece of paper on a flight of stairs can cause you or your child to slip. Don't wax wooden or linoleum stairs and clear away all kinds of extension cords or threadbare rugs. If the stairs lack a guardrail, install one in which the bars are set close enough so that the baby cannot get his head caught between two bars.

In choosing gates, avoid the accordion type in which the baby can easily pinch his fingers or get his head and neck caught between the slats (a number of children have died in this way). Better choices are gates made of plastic mesh or netting. Many such gates are held in place by an expanding bar that exerts pressure against walls or door frames: when installing such a gate, turn the gate so that the pressure bar is *away* from the child. That way he cannot climb on the bar or pry it open. This type of gate is *not* safe enough to be used at the top of a flight of stairs or any other area in the house where falling is a potential hazard.

Two other tips: Check gates frequently to make sure they are properly and securely installed, that all hardware is tight, and that they are locked shut. Even when you have your stairs closed off by gates, you must monitor your child closely. A gate cannot and should not take the place of your own attention.

Checklist of Dangerous or Poisonous Household Objects, Substances, and Plants

Check your floors, cupboards, open shelves, closets, and tabletops for all of these. Whatever you find should be thrown out, locked up, or placed out of reach.

For treatment or choking, poisoning, cuts, or burns, see In Case of Emergency, on p. 000.

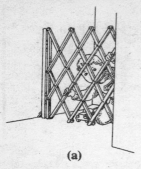

(a) (b)

(a) Avoid accordion-type gates in which fingers or head and neck can get caught.
(b) The preferred gate is made of plastic mesh or netting.

Hazard from Choking or Suffocation

plastic bags
coins
pins
toothpicks
buttons
marbles
paper clips
rubber bands
jewelry, including rings, necklaces, brooches
screws
beads
small batteries including "button" batteries
toys with small pieces (be extra careful if you have a
        toddler and an infant)
latex balloons (Mylar or paper are okay)
sacks of dried peas, beans, corn, etc.
sewing baskets (with pins, needles, buttons, etc.)

Hazard from Cuts, Jabs, or Poking to Eyes or Ears

knives
scissors
forks
toys with long pegs or sharp edges
pens
pencils

Hazard from Poisoning

cigarettes, cigarette butts, ashes (a lit cigarette, cigar, or
    pipe may also burn the baby or be knocked onto
    floor and burn the house)
matches (both poisonous and a fire hazard)
shoe polish
ammonia
bleach
cleaning fluid
scouring powder
furniture polish, waxes, and floor polish and wax
drain cleaners
medications of all sorts (see bathroom baby proofing be-
    low)
pet medications, flea and tick powders and collars
cosmetics
hair spray
shampoo, rinses, dyes
deodorants
leaded paint, turpentine, and paint thinner
batteries
mothballs (poisonous and choking hazard)
kerosene, gasoline, denatured alcohol, lighter fluid

mouse poisons
insecticides
plant sprays and fertilizer
laundry detergents
car cleaners and antifreeze
newspapers
ribbons used in wrapping gifts

Hazard from Burns

lit cigarettes, pipes, etc.
matches
cigarette lighters
stoves, ovens, and wood stoves
hot-water pipes
radiators
space heaters
household hot water (if possible, turn the hot-water ther-
     mostat down to 124° F. to prevent accidental burns
     from tap water)
barbecues
electric fire starters

Hazard from Fire Arms

Each year, forty American children under the age of
four are killed in accidents involving a handgun. To prevent a tragedy with a gun kept in the house:

- Always keep guns and ammunition locked away and
  store them in separate locked places.
- Store the gun unloaded.
- Do not let your child see where the gun is stored.
- Never let children hold or play with guns.

Poisonous Plants

House and garden plants look innocent enough, but in fact they are the number one cause of accidental poisoning for children younger than five. The plants that lead the list of poisonings to children are *philodendron* and *dieffenbachia* (dumb cane)—the latter is so poisonous that a child can burn her mouth just by touching the leaf and then putting her fingers in her mouth.

If you are not sure of the name of a plant, assume it is poisonous and keep it out of reach or out of the house. Hang plants from the ceiling or set them on high shelves; do not put them in children's rooms; never allow a child to play with plants or to use plant leaves as make-believe teacups. As soon as babies are mobile, teach them never to eat or bite plant leaves or stems. Even nonpoisonous plants may be hazards if a baby pulls a heavy flowerpot over on herself or if she eats soils, especially soils treated with fertilizer or insecticide.

Children rarely die from eating small amounts of plant leaves or stems, but they will show symptoms including nausea and vomiting, respiratory difficulty, skin rashes, stomach upset, or dizziness. To treat plant poisoning, see In Case of Emergency, p. 279.

These are the plants we know are poisonous: If you have them in the house, get rid of them or hang them out of reach; if you have them in the garden, fence them off or pull them up. And make sure never to buy them or accept them as gifts.

acorn
amaryllis
asparagus fern
azalea

begonia
bird of paradise (also called poinciana)
black elder
black locust
bleeding heart
boxwood
bunchberry
bulbs (of hyacinth, narcissus, and daffodil)
cactus (spines are a hazard)
caladium
castor bean
cherry laurel
chinaberry
chokecherry
Christmas rose
chrysanthemum
cowslip
creeping fig
crocus
daffodil (bulb)
daphne
deadly nightshade
devil's ivy
dieffenbachia (also called dumb cane)
elderberry
elephant's ear
foxglove
geranium
hemlock
holly berries
hyacinth (bulb)
hydrangea
iris
ivy, including Boston, English, Swedish and poison ivies
jack-in-the-pulpit (leaves)
Japanese yew
Jerusalem cherry

jimsonweed
Jonquil
larkspur
laurel, including mountain, black, sheep, and American
lily of the valley (leaves and flowers)
lobelia
mayapple
milkweed
mimosa (seeds)
mistletoe (berries)
monkshood
moonflower
mushrooms
narcissus (bulb)
oleander (leaves)
oak
philodendron
poison hemlock
poison oak
poison sumac
poinsettia
pokeweed
privet
pyracantha
rhododendron
rhubarb (leaves)
skunk cabbage
sweet pea
Swiss cheese plant (also called Monstera)
tomato (leaves)
Virginia creeper
weeping fig
wisteria (pods)
wild onion
yellow jessamine
yew

Holiday Safety

Holiday season is a time of many injuries to small children because it is a busy time and because many new objects are entering the home. To keep your holiday time safe, remember:

- Hang glass Christmas ornaments (and those with small, breakable pieces) out of reach or put them away until children are older.
- Berries of mistletoe and holly and leaves of poinsettia are poisonous: be careful of these plants at home and out in shops or public displays.
- Christmas trees may be pulled over and electric Christmas lights are a potential hazard, so keep trees in room corners and always monitor children.
- Tinsel may contain lead, so it's safest not to use it unless the package explicitly says no lead.
- Artificial snow is an irritant if inhaled, so keep it away from children.
- Never light a Christmas tree with real candles while young children are around, and always have someone in the room when candles are burning.
- Check over all holiday candy to make sure your child can handle it. Beware of small, round, hard candies and candy canes.

Baby Proofing Your House Room by Room

Nursery

As your baby grows, he'll be spending more and more time playing by himself in his room, so it's especially important that this room is a completely safe place. For tips on furnishing a child's room with safe equipment including crib, toy chest, changing table, and toys, see Chapter 1. Also keep in mind these pointers:

- Shelves must be stable and sturdy so a child cannot pull them over on himself. If necessary, bolt them to the wall.
- Lamps mounted on the wall are safer than table lamps, which have trailing cords that a child could pull or chew on.
- Store safe toys and nontoxic books at your child's level, so he isn't tempted to climb to get them.
- Keep children's rooms reasonably picked up to minimize hazards from tripping over toys.
- Once the baby is climbing, remove the adult-size furniture that he could climb up and fall off of.
- Rocking chairs may pinch a baby's fingers and the runners are easy to trip over. Remove them until the baby is steady on his feet.
- Cool-mist vaporizers are safer than hot-steam vaporizers, but both kinds must be kept up out of a child's reach when they are in use.
- Space heaters are the leading cause of serious burns to young children and are not recommended for home use. If you do use one, keep it out of your child's reach and make sure it's far enough from his crib or bed so that there is no danger of him tossing blankets onto the heater and causing a fire. In particular avoid kerosene heaters. A safer choice of fuel is bottled gas.

Kitchen

Babies love to be in the kitchen because we spend so much time there. Unfortunately kitchens contain more hazards than any other room in the house: hot stoves, pots cooking on top of stove, poisons, cleansers, knives, glasses, and electrical appliances lead the list. With some effort and with scrupulous thoroughness, you can take care of these and make your kitchen safe for baby. However, even the most meticulously baby proofed kitchen should not be a place for wild and rambunctious play. Carolyn, mother of two, recommended fixing up one cor-

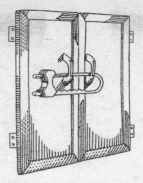

Baby proof cupboards storing dangerous materials with safety latches.

ner of the kitchen for children's play area and enforcing quiet play from the very start.

A lot of parents begin their baby proofing by rearranging their cupboards: they move hazards up to high cupboards and place safe items in lower cupboards where the baby can get at them. *Safe* kitchen items include: wooden spoons, pots and pans, rubber spatulas, rolling pins, potatoes and onions (remove them from plastic bags), hard plastic food-storage containers, paper bags, aluminum pie tins. Stephanie, a mother of a fourteen-month-old girl, made her kitchen safe for play by putting placemats and safe kitchen utensils in lower drawers and moving knives and poisons up to high shelves.

Cupboards and drawers within reach that you don't want the baby getting into can be locked with safety latches. Some varieties fit around the outside of door handles, others attach inside the drawer or cupboard door and prevent the child from pulling them open. If you do install locks or safety latches, *Use them.* Too many of us start off with good intentions and grow careless. If you find yourself getting careless a lot, it's better to move the hazards out of reach so you don't have to worry about

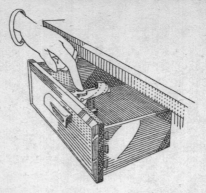

A safety latch that fits inside a drawer or cupboard.

them. You may have to latch lower drawers if the baby uses them to climb to higher drawers.

When baby proofing your cupboards, keep in mind the following:

- Knives, scissors, skewers, forks should all be locked or placed out of reach.
- The cupboard under the sink is a convenient spot to store cleansers, poisons and garbage, and therefore requires special baby proofing. Either move these hazards up to a high shelf or lock the cupboard.
- Keep not only plastic bags, but plastic wrap and foil wrap out of reach (wrap boxes contain sharp cutting edges, and plastic wrap could suffocate a child).
- Be careful about what foods are in reach. Grains, rice, dried beans, and cereals might choke a baby; cans could hurt a baby's feet if dropped.
- Store kitchen matches out of reach and well away from heat sources.

Stove safety is a joint enterprise between you and your children: you should be careful to keep the oven closed

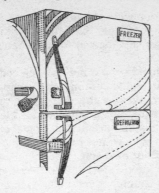

Lock refrigerator doors if necessary.

when it's in use and always to turn pot handles back when cooking; as soon as they become mobile, children should be taught that the stove is a *no* because it's hot. The safest stoves are those with control knobs placed up at the back of the stove where children cannot get at them. If the stove knobs are within reach, see if you can remove them when the stove is not in use. Little ones are great imitators, and if they see us opening oven doors and reaching inside, they may try to do it for themselves. That's why it's so important to explain to them that we're using pot holders to protect ourselves from burns, and that they should not go near the stove because they're too young. Even so, a young child should never be left alone in a kitchen while the oven is on. If necessary, block off the kitchen with gates.

Refrigerator should be arranged so that safe foods are within the child's reach, unsafe foods, breakable bottles, and plastic bags out of reach. Once your child gets big and strong enough, you may have to devise some way of keeping the refrigerator locked shut, either with a latch or with a shock cord through door handles.

It is absolutely essential to remove the doors from un-

used refrigerators when you are storing them. An unused refrigerator is a tempting "play fort" for kids: they climb in, close the door, and then suffocate when unable to open the door again.

Kitchen counters should not have electrical appliances within reach. An eighteen-month-old is capable of pushing a kitchen chair over to the counter, climbing up, and experimenting with toaster, microwave, blender, or whatever. When appliances are in use, you should be there to monitor. When they're not in use, unplug them and put them away and out of reach.

Do not leave knives, forks, or other sharp implements within reach on counter edges. Glasses or cups, especially those containing hot liquids, are also common hazards on kitchen counters.

If you put your baby up on the counter in an infant seat, make sure she is well away from the stove (hot grease can splatter quite a long distance) and that the seat is back from the edge of the counter. Do not leave her unattended.

Kitchen floor should be kept clear of toys, pots, spoons, or other objects that you or your baby could slip on. Wipe up spills as soon as possible. Nonslip floors are the best; hard ceramic tile floors should be avoided if possible. Try to keep the baby from getting underfoot while you're busy preparing or serving a meal. If necessary, put her in a playpen, a high chair, or a crib at crucial moments.

You may have to put the kitchen garbage pail up out of reach until the baby learns not to play in it (or throw things out that you want to keep).

Kitchen table should not be covered with a tablecloth that hangs down within the baby's reach. Tuck trailing edges under. Never hold the baby on your lap while you're drinking hot liquids or eating hot foods that could spill onto her. Do not use your kitchen table (or accessible counters) as a place to store medicines, vitamins, pens, paper clips, etc.

Bathroom

Bathrooms, like kitchens, require extra baby proofing effort because they have so many possible dangers. The two hazards you have to be most careful of here are poisoning and drowning.

Poisoning: Here are some tips for preventing accidental poisonings in the bathroom:

- Put away all potentially dangerous products in a locked medicine cabinet or cupboard. These include all medicines, shampoos, rinses, and dyes, deodorants, cosmetics, nail polish, bathroom cleansers, powders, disinfectants.
- Buy nonprescription drugs in childproof containers and make sure these are properly closed after use. Even childproof containers should be locked away.
- Store prescription medicines only in the labeled containers they came in and follow dosage directions on the label.
- Toss out prescription medicines after use and never give a child medicine that has been prescribed for another child.
- Avoid taking medicines in front of your child. Do not give the child medicines in the dark.
- Never refer to medicine as "candy." Explain that medicines are something *you* give to the child when she's sick, *not* something she takes by herself.
- Do not store medicines in a cabinet over the toilet—this makes access too convenient and tempting.

Drowning: In 1988, 350 children under the age of four died in home-drowning accidents, making drowning the number three cause of accidental childhood deaths, after car accidents and fire (statistics from the National Safety Council). A child can drown in less than two inches of water and it can happen in the time it takes you to answer the door or the telephone. Therefore:

- Never leave a child alone in the bath, even for a moment. If you need to leave, take the child out of the bath, wrap her in a towel, and take her with you.
- Never leave the tub full of water.
- A bath ring or other bathtub restraining device is not a substitute for your constant monitoring: if you use such a device, you *still* must never leave the baby alone in the bath.
- Get in the habit of closing toilet lids.

Other bathroom hazards include electrical appliances such as hair dryers, curling irons, electric razors (all are potential sources of burning as well as electrocution if the child drops the appliance into water in the sink or the tub: if this occurs, unplug the appliance before you pick it up). Unplug and put away appliances as soon as you're finished with them, and don't forget to keep old-fashioned razor blades out of reach as well. Do not let your child play with appliances when they're unplugged to minimize chances that he'll play with them when they are plugged in.

In fact, the bathroom in general is not a place for rough play. There are too many slippery or wet surfaces on which to fall and too many hard surfaces on which to bang the head. One father said he kept toys out of the bath when his kids were in that unruly, early toddler stage so they wouldn't get too wild. To keep bathroom falls to the minimum, put a rubber bath mat or nonskid nonskid stick-ons in the bathtub, use nonskid bath mats on the bathroom floor, and keep the floor as dry as possible. It's also a good idea to install a cushion over the bathtub faucets and spout to protect a child's head in the event of a fall.

When bathing or washing children, always test the bath water (with your wrist or your elbow) to make sure it's not too hot. Don't turn on the hot water and then leave the baby in the tub: wait until the temperature is right before putting the baby in. It may become necessary to attach special devices to the hot-water faucet to keep the baby from turning it on by himself; or you may be able to shut the faucet tightly enough to prevent this.

One good way to keep kids from getting into mischief or danger in the bathroom is to keep the door shut when the room is not in use. Again, this is not a substitute for baby proofing, but an added measure of safety. If your bathroom door can be locked from the inside, either remove the lock or else get in the habit of throwing a towel over the top of the door so that little ones cannot lock themselves in.

Living and Dining Rooms

Fireplaces and wood stoves: The number one hazard in our living rooms are fireplaces and wood-burning stoves. According to statistics compiled by the Consumer Products Safety Commission, in 1989 nearly 3,000 children four years and younger required hospital treatment for accidents related to fireplaces and wood or coal-burning stoves. For baby proofing a fireplace, see the Baby Proofing Checklist (page 38). If possible, position your wood-burning stove in a corner of a room so that you can easily block it off with a gate; or rearrange the furniture in such a way that the stove is barricaded. But even with these precautions, *never leave a child alone in a room while a fire is going in the fireplace or the wood stove.* As with a child in a bath or up on a changing table, you can't run out "just for a second" when a fire is going— that second is when an accident could happen. Take the child with you, put him in his crib or playpen, or ignore the phone, doorbell, whatever.

Falls from furniture: In 1986 some 33,500 children four years old and younger required hospital emergency-room treatment for injuries related to sofas, davenports, divans, and other living-room furniture. There is no way you can keep your child from climbing on the furniture altogether, but you can minimize the risk of injury by:

- Covering all sharp furniture edges with tape-on cushions.
- Discouraging jumping and horseplay on sofas and chairs.
- Removing rickety chairs.
- Positioning favorite sofas and chairs well away from hard coffee tables and other objects on which children could cut or bruise themselves in falls.
- Pushing dining-room chairs in to the table after use.
- Closing chest drawers all the way to keep children from tripping on them or falling into them.

Furniture to Avoid or Protect: Any piece of living-room furniture made of glass, such as a coffee table, an end table, or a lamp, is a potential hazard because a child could break it. Discourage children from playing on or near such pieces, and remove them if necessary.

Stereos, home-entertainment centers, televisions, and other pieces of electronic equipment should also be off-limits. Keep them on high shelves or in locked cabinets.

Bolt to the wall bookshelves, wall units, hutches, and other heavy pieces that a child could pull over on himself.

Long trailing tablecloths on dinning-room tables are irresistible to little ones just learning to pull themselves up. Put away such tablecloths or tuck them in carefully.

Dangerous Ornaments: All of us hate to see our living rooms stripped of glass and pottery decorations, figurines, and other breakable ornaments, but it's far sadder to see a child injured on sharp edges or broken glass (not to mention having the object destroyed). Anything that can break or be swallowed should be removed or put up on a high shelf.

Do Not Leave Lying Around: Matches, cigarette butts, pipes, ashtrays, alcoholic drinks, hot drinks, breakable drinking glasses, bowls of peanuts or candy, cut flowers, cosmetics, pocketbooks, briefcases, ribbons, string, sewing kits.

Apply stickers to picture windows to alert children that they are glass.

Picture Windows: Apply stickers to large picture windows that are down on children's level so they know these are glass. (For more on windows, see Baby proofing Checklist above).

Doors to Outside: Keep outside doors closed and if necessary locked to prevent children from wandering outside unattended.

Utility Rooms

Rooms you use for laundry, sewing, woodworking, indoor gardening, and ironing should be baby proofed along the same lines outlined for the kitchen or the bathroom. Special care must be taken to put laundry detergents up out of reach: detergents are the number one cause of household poisonings.

Be careful not to store the ironing board in a place

where a child could pull it over on himself and never leave a child alone in the room with a hot iron. In fact, even if you're in the room but have your back turned for an instant, a child could pull the iron over on himself by tugging on the cord. So never leave a cord dangling down from the iron, whether it's plugged in or unplugged. Remember that an iron will remain hot long after it's unplugged and that it can cause a serious head wound if it falls.

In many cases it will be impossible to make these rooms really safe for your young children because of the presence of power tools, buttons and needles, sewing machines, etc. In these cases, the best idea is to close off the room, either by keeping the door locked or with a gate. Children tend to be especially curious about the forbidden, so if possible don't let them know that such rooms even exist. In any case, utility rooms should never become play areas for small children and if the little ones do find out about the rooms and become curious, you should explain why they are off-limits.

Baby Proofing Outside the House

Garage

There are two types of possible hazards in the garage—dangerous substances within reach in the garage and the garage doors themselves. Children have been killed when automatically controlled garage doors closed on them, and both automatic and manual doors can crush fingers. If you have automatically controlled garage doors, make sure the control switch is too high for a child to reach and that the remote-control device is locked away from the child. A young child should never be allowed to play alone in the garage. The safest kind of manually operated garage door has a counterbalance system rather than a long coil spring.

As for dangerous substances, our garages and tool-sheds are as bad as kitchens and bathrooms: gasoline and motor oil, garbage cans, old bottles, paint, turpentine, insecticide, power equipment such as lawn mowers and snowblowers, nails, chemical poisons, fertilizers, garden-ing shears—all are items commonly stored in garages and all pose hazards to young children. If you don't have the shelf space to keep all dangerous substances up and out of reach, then close and, if necessary, lock your garage and toolshed when you're not using them.

As an extra safety measure, store gasoline only in con-tainers designed for this use and make sure the container is labeled and kept away from children and from heat sources. There should be no unsupervised children pres-ent when you are using power tools or machinery out-doors.

Patio

One obvious danger on patios and decks is the barbecue. Young children must never be left alone when a barbecue is going, nor should they be present when you are lighting a fire. Both lighter fluid and electric fire starters pose serious hazards to children and to adults as well who use them improperly.

Outdoor furniture is very often unstable and children can easily fall through the slats of woven vinyl or plastic. Falls from lawn furniture onto stone patios or from ele-vated decks are a great deal more serious than indoor falls onto soft carpet. Thus, never let your children climb or play on the lawn furniture. One good way of keeping them off unsteady adult furniture is to buy them their own safe, child-size plastic outdoor furniture.

It is impossible to relax on an open deck with a crawling or toddling youngster. Fence in the deck with mesh fenc-ing material (you can remove it later when children are old enough).

Fold down the barbs on a chain-link fence to minimize the chance of accidents.

See above Checklist of Poisonous Plants for list of plants that should *not* be accessible on your patio or deck.

Yard

Once the little ones are walking, a fence around the yard makes outdoor play a lot easier for you to supervise. Since fences are expensive, you may want to consider fencing in only one section of the yard. Choose wooden fences with rounded and well-sanded fence posts to minimize splinters and chain-link fences on which the barbs at the top are folded down into the fence. Install a gate that closes and latches itself and make sure the latch is three or more feet from the ground. Make sure there are no gaps between the fence bottom and the ground where the child could crawl or wiggle out.

And remember: *a fence alone cannot keep your child safe.* No matter how secure the fence and the gate are,

Outdoor pools should be fenced in.

your child needs adult supervision when playing outdoors.

Another good use of an outdoor fence is to keep children and pets apart in the yard. Children must never be
permitted to play in areas where there are animal feces;
particularly dangerous are feces of puppies that have
worms. Worms, particularly roundworms, can be transmitted to your child through the feces and could lead to
serious infections resulting in brain, liver, and eye damage
and perhaps blindness. Check puppies regularly for
worms and older dogs twice a year and dispose of dog
and cat feces promptly.

If you have a well, a cistern, or a water barrel in your
yard, fence it off and securely cover the top.

Swimming Pool

Pools are a great way to entertain kids on long, hot summer days, but you must be aware of the hazards. According to statistics complied by the Consumer Products
Safety Commission, some 300 children under age five die
each year in drownings in home pools, spas, and hot tubs;
nearly 2000 more children sustain injuries in pool-related
accidents serious enough to require hospital emergency-

room treatment. Even if all you have is one of those inflatable plastic wading pools, *you must never leave a child alone when the pool has water in it*. A drowning could occur in moments in as little as six inches of water.

Permanent pool installations pose greater risks. If you have a pool either inside or outside your home, you must make it inaccessible to children, either by closing off the indoor pool or by fencing the outdoor pool (the fence should be four feet or higher, made of mesh that is no bigger than 2¼ inches, and come equipped with a lock; the safest gates will swing shut and latch by themselves— see above for yard fences. Mary, the mother of a toddler and a newborn, has taken the extra safety precaution of installing an alarm system for her indoor pool: if the door (which is equipped with a lock) is opened or if a child jumps in the water, an alarm will go off. Also, consider these tips for pool safety:

- Apply nonslip material around the pool perimeter.
- Prohibit running in the pool area and horseplay near pool.
- Require all young children to wear life preservers, but do not rely on life preservers to keep children safe.
- Teach children to swim early, but never rely on the swimming prowess of a child to keep him safe in the pool.
- Keep all electrical appliances out of the pool area and hire an electrician to put in ground-fault circuit inter- rupters on all electrical outlets in the outdoor pool area.
- Never bring breakable glasses or plates into the pool area.
- Keep the pool area well-lit when the pool is in use at night.
- Lock away all pool cleaning substances and all electrical pool appliances.

Uncovered pool drains have caused serious injury to children by the strong sucking action they set up as the water drains away. Make sure the pool drain is securely covered by a grate and check the hardware regularly to see that it is tight. Instruct children never to play or sit on the grate and to keep their fingers and their feet away. (For more on pool safety, see Chapter Ten.)

If you have followed every baby proofing suggestion in this chapter, your house is utterly safe for small children upstairs and down, inside and out—and you are utterly exhausted! Don't get overwhelmed by the magnitude of baby proofing chores. Don't plan on doing it all in one day or one weekend. Start a little bit at a time *before* the baby is mobile and get the major baby proofing areas— the kitchen, the bathroom, the stairs, breakables, outlets—taken care of first. After that, tackle the job one room or one cupboard at a time. Stick with it and really focus on it, and the job will be done before you know it.

Of course, once you've got the whole place just right, your child will have cleared another developmental hurdle, grown three inches, learned to climb higher, run faster, and get into places you never dreamed he'd discover—and it will be time to revise and update baby proofing measures and just about every other safety measure, too.

That's what the next section of the book is all about: keeping your growing child safe in the wonderful (and hairraising) toddler years, ages one-and-a-half to three.

Part Two

Expanding Horizons: The Toddler Years, Ages Eighteen Months to Three Years

4. Toddler Safety

In keeping your baby safe, you pretty much ran the show by yourself: you bought the safe equipment and used it safely; you baby proofed the house; you kept track of where your baby was crawling, what she was putting in her mouth, what toys were available to her. But as your more or less controllable and containable baby turns into a head-strong, rambunctious, loquacious toddler, keeping her safe becomes a completely different ball game. In fact, according to the American Academy of Pediatrics, toddlers in the one to two-year-old age-group are the most accident-prone children: fast legs and busy fingers get them everyplace and into everything, but they do not yet have the experience, judgment, or memory to avoid dangers. Victoria, the mother of five sons ranging in age from eight year to thirteen months, agrees with the experts about the high incidence of accidents in the toddler years: "They see someone else do something so they go and do it themselves, not realizing that they might not have the coordination." Common accidents of the toddler years include falls, poisonings, choking on foreign objects, drownings, and burns (car accidents claim the lives of more toddlers than any other kind of accident, but these are accidents that we adults get our children into, not accidents they bring on themselves).

Creating and maintaining a safe environment is as important—or more important—than ever during the toddler years; but childproofing and safe equipment alone are no longer enough. Psychology enters into the picture more and more as you try to steer your child toward safe, appropriate behavior through the mine field of tantrums, resistance, and the urge to do it "my way" or "by self." Nothing is easier than provoking a toddler by firing off a list of imperatives: Never touch that! Don't go there! Be careful! Drop that! But provoking a toddler not only makes you both miserable, but accomplishes next to nothing in terms of safety. Your goal is not to turn safety issues into conflicts, but to make your toddler understand why running into the road is dangerous, why you won't let her pat the neighbor's Doberman, why she must ride in a car seat. Eventually with enough repetition on your part and enough understanding on hers, she will make these safe choices on her own. Maybe not as a two-year-old or three-year-old, but not long after that.

Raising a toddler safely is really a collaboration between the two of you: it requires boundless ingenuity, patience, energy, and love on your side and on your child's part a willingness to cooperate, to listen, to learn. As with all joint enterprises, it's twice as difficult to get both parties to agree, but also twice as rewarding when they do.

Keeping toddlers safe—along with keeping them fed, dressed, entertained, and happy—takes lots and lots of hard work. To help you with the effort of seeing your child safely through the toddler years, keep in mind these general considerations.

Prevent, Don't Confront

If a six-month-old reaches for something unsafe—a cup of hot coffee, a scissors, a bottle of medicine—you can take the object away and he'll forget all about it. A one-year-old in the same situation can usually be distracted by the offer of a safe substitute: his favorite ball for the coffee cup; a game of chase that leads him away from the scissors; a slice of cheese for the medicine bottle. A two-and-a-half-year-old who is denied a coveted object, no matter how hazardous or inappropriate, is a good candidate for throwing a full-scale tantrum. Toddlers have a genius for zeroing in on the *one thing* they cannot or should not have: they can be counted on to find the needle in the haystack, the plastic bag in the playground, the broken glass in the sandbox, the bowl of peanuts on the buffet table. Coaxing often makes them more stubborn. Reason—at least in the heat of the moment—only makes them more unreasonable. If you've ever found yourself *negotiating* with your toddler as he dashes through the house with a carving knife, you know how impossible (and dangerous) the situation can be.

For all of these reasons, it's more important than ever during the toddler years to keep your child's environment as safe as you possibly can. Keep hazards out of sight, out of reach, out of the house and yard altogether and you'll avoid many a tantrum. Accomplishing this goal means meticulous baby proofing (see Chapter 3 for baby proofing and see below for updating your baby proofing for a toddler); forethought about what new objects you bring into the house, where you leave and store things, how you work in the kitchen, the yard, or the laundry room; and careful assessment of any new environment you introduce your toddler to, be it a new playground, friend's house, hotel room. It's also a good idea, particularly with your first child, to try to think ahead about objects or situations that might *become* dangerous a few months down the road. For example, you might think it's cute that your one-year-old has just learned to climb up onto the living-room rocker by himself and so you permit and even encourage him to do so; twelve months later he will be strong enough and wild enough to rock the chair right over onto the floor. Your best bet is to relegate the chair to the attic until the child is able to use it safely.

Similarly never let your child get into the habit of playing with objects that you will eventually have to confiscate, such as sewing kits, medicines, household tools, electrical appliances.

Model Safe Behavior

Children learn a tremendous amount by imitation—including safe habits. If you want your toddlers to behave safely, do so yourself. This means using seat belts in the car, crossing streets with the lights on safe street corners, walking at poolside, not talking, walking, or singing while eating, not using rickety chairs as stepladders, etc. I learned a very good lesson in this area from my two-and-a-half-year-old daughter not long ago. While I was giving her a bath one night, I noticed a huge spider crawling on the ceiling over the tub. Determined to kill it before it escaped, I stood up on the wet side of the tub and leaned precariously forward, balancing with one hand on the ceiling and swatting wildly with the open palm of the other hand. "You know, Dada," my daughter commented as I teetered on the brink of disaster, "that's not a very good thing to do." It wasn't. Luckily she hasn't yet tried this stunt on her own, but she does occasionally give me a funny look when I insist that she sit down in the tub "because it's safer."

Rules, Rewards, and Punishments

Toddlers *need* limits, guidelines, and rules to govern their behavior, and with safety concerns these matters become absolutely vital. The parents I interviewed mentioned these toddler safety rules most frequently:

- Never run into the street.
- Never play with matches, cigarettes, pipes, etc.
- Never touch the stove.
- Never climb on windowsills or play with window screens.
- Never touch the fireplace or barbecue, even when they are not in use.
- Never play with electrical appliances; never unplug or plug in appliances.
- Never ride in the car without the car seat.
- Never enter a pool or pool area unsupervised.
- Never go outside without getting permission.
- Never play alone in bathrooms.

Making rules is one thing, but getting your toddler to obey them is quite another. "They listen, but it's difficult for them to stick to rules," said Marilu, the mother of two toddler girls in North Bergen, New Jersey. "We still have to keep an eye on them." Though you can't yet expect a toddler to remember and obey your rules consistently, you still need to set rules in all major safety areas, to explain the rules carefully and clearly, and to follow through with some sort of action when the rules are broken. Don't just say "No!" to the toddler who is heading for the street: pick him up and take him away. When setting rules, explain to your toddler *why* you have made the rule and why it's important. Wanda, the mother of a three-year-old boy, gave him a demonstration of what would happen if he didn't wear his car seat: while driving slowly with him on a lonely country road, she braked suddenly and showed him how all the letters on the front seat went flying to the floor. "After that he was more cooperative about using his car seat," she said. Carol tells her toddlers that they have to buckle up just the way Mommy and Daddy do.

Once the rule is set, apply and enforce it consistently; if you waffle or overlook infractions, your child will start to think that you don't really "mean it" and will be more likely to give you a hard time the next time you try to enforce it. Don't worry about repeating the rule endlessly: repetition is the way children learn. Some parents get in the habit of stating the rule *every time* they confront the potential danger; some turn rules into songs or rhymes. Eventually the toddler may take over the job of repeating the rule. Once a rule is set, you can discuss it with your toddler and answer any questions he might have; but try to avoid getting trapped into making exceptions, bargaining over fine points, or getting yourself maneuvered onto the witness stand. ("Why is it okay for *you* to throw logs on the fire and not *me*?") Occasionally you may have to resort to that tired but still useful parental formula: "Because I'm a grown-up, and grown-ups can do things like this."

In explaining rules, stress the positive side and don't dwell on the gory consequences of breaking safety rules. For example, you might say, "You must always ride your tricycle with one of us watching you and you must only ride on the side of the road so you will be out of the way of fast cars," rather than, "If you ride in the middle of the road, you could be hit by a car and die." Horror stories will only frighten and confuse little ones.

No matter how long the rule has been in effect and how well your toddler seems to abide by it, always keep in mind that you can't trust a toddler to remember and obey on his own. As Fitzhugh Dodson and Ann Alexander put it in their book *Your Child: Birth to Age Six*: the toddler "lives in only one kind of time: the eternal *now*. She can neither make nor break a promise, for she cannot truly remember the past or plan for the future." Many toddlers enjoy demonstrating how obedient they are and how accurately they can parrot back rules as long as you are with them: but the instant you turn your back, the urge to see for themselves whether the barbecue is really hot or how the car's hand brake works becomes too powerful to resist. Thus even if you have set down clear and consistent rules, you must continue to supervise and monitor a toddler through any potentially dangerous situation. You can't really expect your child to remember and obey rules on his own until he reaches the preschool years, and even then you must assess both the situation and the child's maturity carefully.

When a toddler breaks a safety rule, he must suffer some sort of consequence, otherwise the rule is just a lot of hot air. Always try to make the punishment fit the crime—and save your punishments for when you really need them. A punishment for a minor infraction—for example, standing up in the bath or rocking in a high chair— can be a sharp "No!" and, if the unsafe behavior stops, you can leave it at that. If your toddler continues to break the safety rule, pick her up and remove her from the scene of the "crime." You might explain why she is being reprimanded, for instance, "You know you are not supposed to climb on the glass table because it could break and you could cut yourself. Don't do it again."

Lots of parents have had good results with a punishment called "time-out." The essence of "time-out" is removing the child from the fray and isolating her from you and from the rest of the family for a short time. When you decide she needs "time-out," pick her up (preferably facing away from you so she doesn't think she is getting a hug) and carry her off to some safe place where you can leave her alone without worrying about her for a short time. One child-care expert recommends a minute of "time-out" for every year of age starting at age two. As you carry out the punishment, explain, "I'm giving you

time-out because you were playing with matches...
reaching for the knives...running at the pool, or whatever—and you know that's dangerous." Once the time is
up (if you want to be exact, you can set the kitchen timer),
let the toddler rejoin the family but, if possible, keep her
away from the situation or object that got her into trouble.
After the toddler has served her "sentence" let the matter
drop: this is not the time to launch into a speech about
the dangers of whatever. The "time-out" has made the
point more eloquently than a lecture would.

"Time-out" is probably the most serious punishment
you will want to use to correct a toddler who is breaking
safety rules. Hitting or verbally abusing a child is *not* an
effective way of enforcing rules and, in fact, hitting a child
may be as unsafe as any misbehavior on the child's part.
All too often we hear of parents who have hurt their
children by hitting them in the heat of the moment. One
virtue of "time-out" is that it gives both of you an opportunity to cool off. A good deal of toddler misbehavior
is the result of ill-guided bids for attention: negative attention is better than no attention at all in the mind of the
toddler. "Time-out" deprives the toddler of that attention
and thus teaches her that the more she breaks the rules
the less attention she will get. Hitting a toddler teaches
her mostly to resent and fear her parents.

Just as we correct and punish our toddlers when they
break our safety rules, so we should praise and reward
them when they abide by the rules. A toddler who has
stayed close to his parents during a long shopping trip,
avoided running out into the parking lot, ridden obligingly
in his car seat on a long drive, and sat quietly through the
meal in a rickety restaurant booster seat deserves some
sort of award. Toddlers appreciate praise, thanks, or special attention as much as the rest of us: it costs you nothing
to tell your toddler how proud you are of him for being
good and it means a lot to him. For more major feats of
good behavior, some parents use star charts, some hand
out treats or gifts, and some reward a toddler with a spe-

cial activity—a bubble bath, an extra trip to the park, a bike ride, or whatever makes the child feel special.

Draw Your Battle Lines Carefully

Given how negative, impulsive, and self-willed the average toddler can be, you may find yourself slipping into a rut in which you spend nearly all your time correcting and punishing the child. Jeri, the mother of three girls, ages ten, three, and one, in Elkhart, Indiana, said when she stopped to count how many times she said "no" in the course of a day "it was overwhelming," so overwhelming that she made a special effort to correct it. Jeri and her husband sat down and looked at the situation in a calmer moment and narrowed down the battles to only the most serious situations.

There are some battles that are worth fighting and others that are not. The issue of safety makes some of these decisions considerably more clear-cut. Compromise is out of the question on any behavior that could result in a serious accident—playing with sharp or pointed objects; eating foods or mouthing toys the toddler could choke on (anything small, round, smooth, or slippery; see Chapter 2 for a list of forbidden foods for babies—most of the same foods should still be avoided); riding out of the car seat; playing on steps. But with a toddler you can begin to relax certain safety rules that you enforced a few months back. Since a toddler is surer on his feet than a baby just learning to walk, he can probably begin to negotiate steps alone (as long as you hover a couple steps down to catch him) and he can be trusted to climb up the low slide in the playground. If he goes wild when you try to strap him into a high chair, you could forget the strap or switch to a booster seat; a large, agile toddler may be allowed to climb out of the bath himself with your close supervision. When Jeri's middle daughter was two, she showed absolutely no fear of the water and in fact would repeatedly jump off the side of the pool and go under; Jeri knew this could be dangerous, so she supervised the toddler particularly closely whenever they were at the pool. Rather than deal with an argument, Marilu lets her three-year-old unload the knives from the dishwasher, keeping a close eye on her all the while. Marge allows her three-year-old to cut pictures out of magazines with adult scissors. Wanda occasionally lets her three-year-old play with certain tools, for example screwdrivers, again with supervision; she also tries to use the occasion to teach him the difference between tools you *use* and toys you *play with*.

I'm not suggesting that you encourage unsafe behavior or even overlook it; but rather that you let your toddler have his way in the situations that won't get him into serious trouble. This is really a matter of individual judgment based on what you can tolerate, how closely you can supervise, and how your child behaves. Some children are more accident prone than others and need more guidance; others can be turned loose with less concern. All children improve steadily in balance, manual dexterity, and the ability to understand, remember, and carry out verbal commands during the course of toddlerhood. Try to recognize your child's progress and gradually back off in some of the less crucial safety issues.

Keep in mind as well that making too many rules may backfire by leading your toddler into temptation. "There are some things he must learn by experience," said one mother of her toddler son. "He has been given freedom within guidelines." Victoria, who has five sons, has discovered other drawbacks to making too many rules: "When you have a giant checklist of rules, *you* forget what the rules are, but *they* don't and they're always testing to see what you'll do. It's better to have simple rules that you will follow through on, not lots of little ones." Also, overdoing it on rules might actually give your toddler ideas for misbehavior. It might never have occurred to him to play in the laundry room, throw wooden blocks at his younger brother, or experiment with nibbling the houseplants until you made these activities off-limits. So remember: don't pick fights when you can possibly avoid them and don't create problems where none exist.

Childproofing Update

The baby proofing that you carried out with such scrupulous care and patience when your infant began to crawl is unfortunately no longer adequate. Your toddler is bigger, more active, more agile, more inventive, more determined, more curious, and better able to satisfy her curiosity than she was as a baby. Thus to keep her safe at home and outdoors, you're going to have to update your childproofing. Remember as a general rule to move all hazardous substances and equipment several feet higher to keep them out of your toddler's reach. Also remember that a toddler is perfectly capable of pulling a chair or stool over to the cabinet or closet that contains some forbidden object and thus boosting her reach by two or three feet more. Locked cabinets and top shelves are essential for storage.

Review the baby proofing suggestions in Chapter 3 and then consider the following points to bring your childproofing up to the level of your growing child.

Kitchen and Bathroom Cabinets and Drawers:

Toddlers can reach drawers and cabinets that were too high for babies;, toddlers may be able to figure out some cabinet latches and undo shock cords. Test all baby proofing hardware to see how well it has stood up and to assess whether it is still adequate.

Kitchen and Bathroom Countertops:

Greater height gives toddlers access to counters they previously couldn't reach. Be especially careful about leaving knives, containers of hot liquid, razors, or electrical appliances near the edges of counters. Many toddlers, seeing the edge or handle of an object on a counter, will reach for it and pull it down on themselves.

Cords on Blinds or Curtains:

Similarly these must be kept up even higher so a toddler cannot reach them or get the cord looped around his neck. You may have to wind up dangling cords and secure them with a twist or rubber band (be careful that the rubber band does not fall on the floor—your toddler could choke on it if he gets it in his mouth). Check that blinds are installed securely so there is no danger of them falling onto a child's head.

Stove:

A toddler is more at risk than an infant because he can reach higher and may even try opening the oven door in imitation of you. It is vital to protect your toddler from the stove: remove the control knobs from the stove when you are not using it and when either the oven or the top burners are on make sure you supervise your toddler at all times. Remember: cook on the back burners when possible and always turn pot handles to the back of the stove. Continue telling your toddler that the stove is *hot* and that he must never touch it.

Bath Safety:

Because your toddler is sturdier and steadier than he was as a baby, you may be tempted to leave him alone

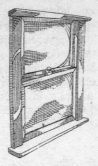

As your child gets bigger, windows may have to be locked and covered with safety screens.

in the bathtub or wading pool "just for a minute" while you run to the door, to the phone, or to search for a favorite bath toy. *Don't do it*. If you must leave the room *always* wrap up your child in a towel and take her along. A toddler can drown just as quickly and in just as little water as a baby. Control bathtub play so that your toddler does not get too wild and run the risk of falling and hurting himself. Check the nonskid stickers in your tub to make sure they have not been worn smooth.

Furniture with Sharp Edges:

As your child grows, you will have to protect him from the sharp edges of furniture that he once could walk or crawl under without danger.

Go through the house and, if necessary, measure the height of various pieces. Cover any sharp edges with cushioned adhesive tape.

Windows:

Similarly windows that were once too high to pose any danger may have to be locked and covered with safety screens now that your child is bigger. In New York City it has been mandatory since 1976 for owners of apartment buildings where children age ten and under live to install window guards on all windows except those opening on fire escapes. If you have double-hung windows, open accessible windows from the top only. It's more important than ever to apply stickers to large floor-to-ceiling picture windows and glass doors so that your active toddler will not accidentally crash into them.

Doors to the Outside:

A toddler with wanderlust is perfectly capable of letting himself out the front door of your house and heading out into the world while your back is turned. If your toddler has the impulse to explore, you may have to install an inside key lock or put a bolt lock or hook high enough so that the toddler cannot reach it.

If you have installed such a lock, remember to use it.

Outlet Covers:

A toddler may be able to pry off some brands. If this happens, buy a different type and keep experimenting until you find one that works.

Safety Gates:

The hardware may have worked itself loose on the gates you installed for your baby; check all screws and nuts and tighten them if necessary. Make sure the gates you use are sturdy enough to withstand the greater force and weight of a toddler. Even though your older toddler can probably go up and downstairs by himself, you should still be there to supervise him. Thus it's as important as ever to keep safety gates latched across both the top and the bottom of flights of steps when you are unable to keep an eye on your child.

Poisonous Plants:

The same household and garden plants that could poison a baby can poison a toddler, and a toddler can reach or climb to many more plants than a baby can. Review the list of poisonous plants in Chapter 3. You may have to move houseplants to an even higher shelf or hang them from the ceiling. A toddler is more likely than a baby to roam around in the yard and use leaves, stems, and flowers in imaginative play; thus protecting him from unsafe garden plants is essential. If you haven't already fenced in your yard or part of your yard, this may be the time to do it (see Chapter 3 for guidelines on buying and installing fences). Don't invite trouble by assuming that unknown plant species are safe: bring a sample to your local nursery and find out what it is. If you don't want to uproot unsafe plants, you're going to have to take measures to insure that your child does not touch or eat them, such as fencing them off or supervising your child's play constantly.

Power Tools:

Toddlers love to "help" with outdoor chores and gardening, but their helping becomes extremely hazardous when you are operating power tools. Toddlers should *not* be in the yard with you when you are using lawn mowers, chain saws, snow or leaf blowers and other power tools.

A Wider Range of Exploration:

A one-year-old is unlikely to ascend the stairs to the attic while you are busy washing the dishes, but you can almost count on your two-year-old to do just that. As your little explorer grows bolder and more adventurous, you'll have to extend the range of your childproofing. Attics and basements should be securely locked at all

Use a toddler car seat once your child weighs twenty pounds.

times. Lock or dispose of large trunks, coolers, and hampers that your toddler could climb or fall into.

Equipment Update

As your child grows taller, heavier, and stronger, you will need to review the basic equipment you have been using to make sure it is still safe. In some cases you will have to retire baby equipment or pass it down to a new baby brother or sister; other pieces of equipment remain safe so long as your toddler agrees to use them safely. Check through these items for safety:

Car Seats:

Once your child weighs twenty pounds, you must retire her infant car seat and acquire a toddler car seat, which will keep her safe in the car until she reaches sixty pounds. Or, if you have been using a convertible-type car seat from the start, you can continue using it for your toddler: you convert the seat from infant to toddler use by turning it to face forward, making sure to refasten the seat prop-

**You may switch to shell booster seat when your child
reaches thirty pounds. To make it even safer, attach a
harness to the back seat of your car.**

erly with the car seat belts and raising and loosening the
straps (see Chapter 1 for a discussion of infant and convertible car seats).

When purchasing a toddler car seat, make sure the seat
was manufactured after January 1, 1981 (check for a label
with date of manufacture), for strict federal guidelines
went into effect on this date. The safest type of toddler
seat is a shell seat, which is basically the same thing as
a convertible seat adjusted to the toddler position. Later
on, when your toddler weighs over thirty pounds, you
may want to pass on the shell seat to a younger sibling
and put her in a harness-type seat, which is rather like a
booster seat with a chest and shoulder harness that you
must attach to your car. The shell seat is safer, so there
is no reason to move her up to a harness-type seat unless
you have to.

The safest position for a toddler car seat, as for an infant
or convertible seat, is in the middle of the car's backseat.
But if you must place the seat close to one of the car
doors, *be extra careful when you close the door that your
toddler's fingers are not in the way.* Children have lost
fingers when car doors were slammed on them. In addition, if the child's seat is next to a door, a toddler who
is not buckled into his seat could fall out of the car when

the door is opened—a potentially serious accident even when the car is parked. So when you stop your car, leave your toddler buckled up until you can get out of the car, walk around to his door, and lift him out.

Toddlers may be able to unsnap or unbuckle the restraints on their car seats, so you should keep a close eye out for this. If it happens repeatedly and punishment (see above) doesn't correct the problem, you may have to invest in another seat that is more childproof.

High Chairs and Hook-on Seats:

If you can't get your toddler to sit quietly in her high chair, it's time to move her to a booster seat or to the old stack of telephone books. A very rambunctious toddler can wriggle out of her high-chair strap in no time, and once she's out of the strap, she's at serious risk of slipping out of the high chair or toppling it over. So rather than take the chance, retire the high chair. Similarly the hook-on seat should be retired when your toddler reaches thirty pounds or when she begins to bounce or rock in the seat. A determined toddler can shake her hook-on seat loose from the table and plummet seat and all to the floor in the time it takes you to say "pass the butter."

Crib and Bed:

You'll probably want to keep your child in her crib as long as possible simply for the convenience of it, but circumstances may dictate switching her to a bed earlier than you had intended. If you are expecting another child, you will most likely want the crib for the new baby; or your toddler may have figured out how to climb out of her crib and begin each day by crashing from the top crib rail to the floor. If this is the case, your toddler is better off in a bed, provided the bed is low to the ground. Until your child stops rolling around so much, use only a mat-

Use a bed guard to keep him from rolling out of bed while sleeping.

tress on a box spring. For added protection you can buy a bed guard, which is a safety rail that runs the length of the bed and keeps the child from rolling out. Even with a bed guard, toddlers have been known to roll off the ends of their beds—so it's a good idea to keep the floor all around the bed clear and perhaps in the first months of bed-sleeping to line the floor with pillows or cushions.

Playpen:

As soon as your child is able to climb out of the playpen, it's time to put it away. The Consumer Products Safety Commission has issued a warning about the accordion-type baby enclosures (a portable corral that parents use at home or in the yard to confine children).

Accordion-type baby enclosures are dangerous. A child could entrap his head or neck and strangle.

These enclosures, like the unsafe type of baby gates (see Chapter 3), have V and diamond-shaped openings in which a child could entrap his head or neck and strangle. If you have this type of enclosure, get rid of it. Discontinue using any type of child enclosure when your child is large enough to knock it over or climb out. And avoid playpens with fishnet-type netting in which your child can entangle his fingers, toes, or buttons on his clothes.

Toys:

The same general guidelines for choosing baby toys apply to choosing toys for toddlers—see Chapter One for a detailed discussion of toy safety. As your toddler grows, she will play more actively and even roughly with her toys, so check through them periodically for wear and tear. Throw out any toys with sharp edges, splinters, or small parts that could come off. Electrical or battery-operated toys should only be permitted when you can be there to supervise. At holiday and birthday times try to make safe toy suggestions to relatives and friends so you can avoid battles over confiscating hazardous toys. The age recommendations marked on toy packages are not always a good guideline: every child matures at a different rate and your child may not be ready at the age the toy manufacturer thinks he should be. If you have a new baby in the house, you should carefully go through your toddler's toys (preferably when she is not around) and remove any that could be potentially dangerous to the baby. Carol, the mother of a four-year-old and two-year-old twins (all boys), said that once the twins began to crawl she only let her older son play with his small Legos, tinker toys, crayons, and matchbox cars when she could supervise or when the twins were napping.

In a pamphlet entitled "Think Toys Safety," The Consumer Products Safety Commission recommends that parents ask the following questions about the toys they buy and accept for their toddlers:

- Is the plastic strong enough to endure rough play?
- Does the toy shoot or throw out objects that could injure a child's eyes?
- Does the toy make a loud noise that could damage a child's hearing?
- If the toy comes wrapped in plastic, have you safely disposed of the plastic wrap?
- If the toy comes in a box or crate, is the container safe enough to leave in your child's room?[illustrate]?
- Do you gather up all toys used in the yard or park at the end of the day to prevent them from rusting?

There is no question that toddlerhood taxes our patience, our imaginations, our wills, and our energy to the limit and sometimes beyond the limit. Keeping a toddler safe can sometimes seem like a running battle with a dynamo who is determined to self-destruct. There may be times when even the most devoted parent wistfully recalls the "good old days" of babyhood when every attention was met with smiling cooperation, when keeping the baby safe could be as simple as popping her in her crib or playpen while we changed the laundry, answered the phone, or opened the oven door. Life was so simple then and safety so straightforward. But it's important to remember that difficult and demanding as toddlers sometimes are, they can also be a good deal more fun and rewarding to be with than babies for the simple reason that they can say and do and understand more. With increased mental and physical abilities comes a wide new range of activities and situations that your toddler will explore. As your toddler's horizon expands, so does your role in keeping her safe. The next two chapters cover keeping your toddler safe and making your toddler *aware* of safety through all the new endeavors she will pursue.

5. New Situations

A toddler can, within the limits of her nap schedule, her attention span, and her temper, go just about anywhere you go. The supermarket, the shopping mall, trains, buses, and subways are for her great adventures. The playground is her magic kingdom and her arena of discovery. Restaurants are like quick trips to exotic countries and a night or two in a motel is like a voyage into outer space, but even a walk or a tricycle ride around the block can be a treat. From the toddler's perspective, the world around her is like a Garden of Eden without the serpent; recognizing and protecting her from the serpent (along with all the other pitfalls and hazards of the world) is your job. If you do your job well, you will protect her without spoiling her wonderment—and you may even lead her to take her first steps toward looking out for herself.

Protecting your toddler from the potential hazards of her new activities is a good deal easier if you are prepared in advance—if you know what to expect and have given some forethought as to how to minimize risks or avoid them altogether. This chapter contains a rundown of the new situations and activities that your toddler is likely to encounter and how you can guide her safely through them.

Public Places

Playgrounds:

For a toddler, a playground means freedom, but this is not always so for a toddler's parent. It would be great if all playgrounds were totally safe, clean, hazard-free environments—but on second thought, maybe that would take some of the fun out of it. In any case, playgrounds have their dangers and parents of toddlers should be aware of them, especially during the first few visits when they may not be familiar with the equipment, the other children, or their own child's capabilities and limitations. When first visiting the playground, it makes good sense to inspect the equipment for sharp corners, rusty edges, splinters, loose boards or joints, and tight spaces in which your toddler could get her head caught. Playground equipment standing on hard concrete is potentially much more hazardous than equipment standing on sand, grass, or wood chips. Playground sand may conceal broken glass, bottle caps, cigarette butts, animal feces, and other harmful substances: again, take a good look before you let your child loose. If the playground doesn't meet these basic safety standards, find a better one, rally the parents in your community to make changes, or invest the money in a well-made swing set for your own yard.

Also check playgrounds for these safety features:

- The equipment should be securely anchored into concrete or the ground.
- A fenced-in playground makes minding the children easier for you.
- Hanging rings should be either smaller than five inches in diameter or larger than ten to prevent possible strangulation.

- Seesaws pose a number of problems for young children: the fulcrum can pinch fingers; children may catch their legs under the board when it touches the ground; a child can be hurled off the seat or crash to the ground if his partner dismounts without warning him. For all of these reasons seesaws are not really appropriate for children this age.
- Slides should be a maximum of six feet high; metal slides should be shaded from the sun; children should slide into soft material such as sand or sawdust that is free of debris.

No one likes to hover over an active, independent-minded toddler at the playground, but you must do *some* hovering until you determine your child's abilities. After that, lay down certain playground rules and make sure your toddler obeys them. High slides are a real hazard for falls, and a toddler can get seriously hurt by falling off a swing or a merry-go-round. One at a time is a good rule for slides and it's wise to teach your child to stand up and move away as soon as she reaches the bottom of the slide. You'll have to remind your toddler over and over not to wander too close to swings, and it's a good idea to be near at hand to grab her out of the way if she's the stubborn type who won't listen. Teach your toddler to hold on to the swing with both hands and not to kneel, stand, or jump off the swing.

At the playground, your toddler will raptly observe the antics of older children and immediately try to copy them. This requires your special attention: toddlers do not know the limits of their strength and coordination and may get themselves into serious trouble when they try to copy five-year-olds by letting go on the merry-go-round or climbing to the top of the jungle gym. When I take my three-year-old daughter to the playground, I act as her "spotter": I try to let her explore things on her own without making a big fuss about the dangers, but I'm there in case she falls off the fire truck or goes flying off the parrot on the spring coil.

Rare is the playground that doesn't have its resident bully—or bullies. Dealing with toy grabbers is really a matter of personal choice and temperament, but you should not leave your toddler to fend for himself if another child is hitting, swinging toy rakes or shovels around, or throwing sand. Try to get the bully's parent to put a stop to the behavior and by all means take your toddler out of the line of fire.

Pools:

Public swimming pools, even wading pools meant for little ones, offer one very obvious hazard: drowning. According to statistics complied by the National Safety Council, in 1986, 300 children under age five died in drownings in public places, and 400 children in this age-group died in drownings at home. To repeat the admonition offered earlier about bathtubs: a child can drown in as little as six inches of water and it can happen in minutes. So to be safe at the pool: supervise your toddler at all times even if there is a lifeguard on duty.

Lots of parents will exempt themselves from this rule because they have strapped water wings, swim sweaters, inflatable rings, or life preservers to the toddlers. However, many safety experts issue very strong warnings about such devices precisely because they create a false sense of security. Most toddler flotation devices will buoy the child's arms or body up but will actually push her face into the water. Though the child is floating, she will suffocate nonetheless in the water. But even the most carefully designed life preservers do not offer a safe substitute for constant parental monitoring at poolside. *A life preserver or inflatable tube alone is not enough to keep a toddler safe at the pool.*

Parents of toddlers have also been lulled into a false sense of security by enrolling their children in swimming classes. There has been a lot of excitement in recent years at the discovery that very young children—even infants—can be taught to swim. If your child shows an interest and enjoys the class, by all means enroll him (see box on Infant and Toddler Swim Classes). The right kind of class will do your child no harm (though it may do him little or no long-term good). But even if he graduates at the head of his swim class and the instructor feels he is future Olympics material, your toddler cannot be trusted alone in the water. No toddler has the judgment, the stamina, or the ability to swim unsupervised, even in a wading pool. And of course, the larger the pool, the more careful you must be.

Poolside safety is also an important consideration. As a general practice, you should forbid running and rough horseplay at poolside, and no diving either. Permitting a toddler to enter or play near a lake, bay, or ocean without you being right there holding onto him is simply inviting trouble. So don't do it.

Infant and Toddler Swim Classes: The Pros and Cons

The idea of a six- or twelve-month-old baby dog-paddling competently across a pool once seemed utterly fantastic—but no more. A number of books (including *Teaching an Infant to Swim* by Virginia Hunt Newman, Harcourt Brace Jovanovich, 1967 and *Infant Swimming* by Cynthia Clevenger, St. Martin's Press, 1986) and a bit of hoopla in the popular press have spread the news that very young children can be taught to swim. But now that the "water-babies" fad has subsided a bit, a clearer picture is emerging on the subject of young children in the water. Before enrolling your infant or toddler in a swim class, keep in mind these very important points:

- A class may teach your infant or toddler to swim, but that does not mean that he can handle himself unsupervised or that he can deal with an emergency. *No child under the age of ten should be left alone near the water, and no child (or adult) should ever swim alone.*

- Conservative water-safety authorities recommend age three as the time to begin a child's swimming lessons. Though younger children have been taught to swim, many parents say that their one- and two-year-olds forget their swimming skills soon after the classes end.

- So-called "drown-proofing" classes contain a contradiction in their very title: No child and certainly no child under age three can be "drown proofed." Such classes, and in fact all infant and toddler swimming classes, may pose the very serious risk of giving parents a false sense of security about their child's abilities in the water. No one—child or adult—is "drown proof."

- The American Academy of Pediatrics (AAP), the National YMCA, and the Council for National Cooperation in Aquatics now oppose swim classes that use forced-submersion techniques (letting the child go under, throwing him in the water, or blowing water repeatedly in his face). Quite aside from the cruelty of these techniques, there is a risk that children who have been subjected to them will develop "water intoxication" by swallowing too much water. The symptoms are lethargy, vomiting, and even seizures. Besides, such sink-or-swim techniques may make a child scared of the water for a long time.

- For a toddler, your best choice is probably a swim class that emphasizes water safety and water play rather than swimming skills or drown proofing. Look for classes in which all the children receive one-to-one supervision. The AAP has issued a strong warning to parents to avoid classes featuring group swimming instruction for children under three.

- Don't rush your toddler into swim classes. Wait until the child shows an interest. Parents commonly report that their children begin to fear the water after unhappy experiences in swim classes.

Stores, Malls, and Supermarkets:

Most toddlers are enthusiastic shoppers: the activity, the colors and shapes of all the products, the opportunity to get out and experience new environments are much more exciting to them than any practical considerations you might have. But with the excitement of shopping comes the increased risk that your toddler might wander off, fall behind, or get separated from you. Most parents of toddlers I talked to said that a stroller was absolutely essential for safe shopping trips. Carol, the mother of twin toddler boys, said she ventured into a store without a stroller recently. "It was a big mistake. As soon as I put them down, the twins ran all over the store. I'll never do that again." (For more on keeping twins safe, see the box below.) Carol has found that a double stroller is the only way to transport her twins, and Marilu, whose toddler daughters are only ten months apart, also uses one. However, Marilu cautions that double strollers are very difficult to manage and in many stores she can't maneuver the stroller up and down the aisles. Her rule is, "If the stroller doesn't fit, I won't go in that store."

In supermarkets, the best way to keep track of your toddler is to let him ride in the shopping cart. Unfortunately not all toddlers are willing to do this. One mother of a three-year-old, lets him push the cart with one hand if he promises to hold onto her hand or leg with his other hand. Marge, a Fort Lauderdale mother of two sons, said the only time she had trouble keeping track of her children in stores was when she went to a large hardware store that had no shopping carts. "My toddler just took off and kept going down the aisles. Several cashiers saw him go by, but no one thought to stop him. After that experience, I told him to stay put or go to the cash register if he gets separated. 'If you stand where you are, I'll find you,' I told him. 'Just don't keep running.'"

Holding hands in stores and malls can be one of your safety rules. If your toddler is reluctant, you might buy a "hand-holder," which is like a coiled phone cord that attaches you to your toddler by the wrist. This is certainly a more appealing way to keeping track of your children than putting them on leashes or in harnesses. Many parents find that it simply isn't possible for a single adult to handle more than two young children in stores or malls. If you have a large family, try to schedule your shopping trips on weekends so you can go with your spouse or enlist the help of grandparents or even a willing teenager.

Fitzhugh Dodson and Ann Alexander make an excellent suggestion for teaching toddlers public safety in their book *Your Child Birth to Age 6*. They recommend taking little ones on "practice outings," little trips to the shopping center, museum, restaurant, whatever, that you make for the express purpose of instructing them in how to behave safely in new situations. Dodson and Alexander suggest that you explain the necessary safety precautions beforehand (for example, never let go of Mom's hand or purse strap; no running or shouting in a museum or library; no grabbing things off store shelves) and then praise and reward them when they obey the rules. It's a good idea to explain to a toddler exactly what you are praising him for—"I'm glad you held my hand in the shop; that way you didn't get lost"—instead of just saying, "You were a very good boy today . . . " One advantage of the practice outings is that you are really focusing on your child's needs and abilities, rather than on accomplishing your own shopping or whatever. Your child will enjoy the attention, you will gain a very clear idea of how he behaves himself, and when you do take him on a "real" shopping trip, you will know what to expect and he will be more familiar with the situation and with your safety rules.

If Your Toddler Gets Lost in a Public Place

It's best to prepare your toddler by discussing with her—not once, but repeatedly—what to do in case she gets lost or separated from you in public.

- Tell your toddler to stay put: that way you can easily retrace your steps and find her.
- Tell your toddler to notify a policeman (show her a policeman and point out the blue uniform and cap), security guard, park attendant, store clerk (point out the people who work behind the cash registers or the people who wear identifying name tags) that she is lost.
- Teach your toddler to memorize her full name, address, and phone number and your full names (this will take some time, but stay with it and she'll learn). You might also slip a card with this information into her pocket and tell her to show it to a policeman, security guard, or store clerk.
- Teach your toddler not to go off with anyone except a uniformed police officer. If anyone else tells your toddler to come with him, your child should reply, "I'm waiting here for my mother or father." (For more on discussing safety in public, see Chapter 6.)
- Once you discover your toddler is missing, carefully retrace your steps, notifying store clerks, museum guards, or whoever might help in each location that your toddler is missing. Describe the child and tell them when you realized she was missing. If you do not locate the child quickly, notify the police.
- The sooner you notify the police, the better the chances are that your toddler will be found quickly.
- After you have called the police, make sure someone is at your home to answer the phone or to receive the child in case she makes her way back.

To help you begin explaining to your toddler how to behave if she gets lost or separated in public, you might want to get hold of a very good children's book called *Don't Worry, I'll Find You* by Anna Grossnickle Hines (Dutton, 1986). Using a simple story and pictures that a toddler can easily understand and relate to, the book teaches children to stay put if they become separated from their parents in public places.

Safety With Twins

Raising twins safely has its own special demands, and the toddler period is probably the time when these demands will be most pressing. "The biggest problem with twins," says Shirley Maag, first vice president in charge of education for the National Organization of the Mothers of Twins Club, "is when they hit that curious stage and one goes in one direction and the other goes in the opposite direction. It's important to keep an eye on both children, but sometimes it's impossible."

Ms. Maag and other parents of twins (including myself) offered these tips for safety:

- Use a playpen for as long as your twins will tolerate it and stay in it. Once they learn to climb out, it's time to put the playpen away. (For information on buying a safe playpen, see Chapter 1.)
- Make sure your twins do not have toys with which they can hurt each other: hard wooden blocks or sharp plastic objects should be avoided.
- A double stroller, though essential for outings with twins, is much more difficult than a single stroller to maneuver in stores, on crowded sidewalks, and in other public places. A double stroller with the seats side-by-side will *not* fit on many elevators and will pose a greater hazard than a single stroller if you are strolling on streets without sidewalks. A front-to-back stroller is a safer and more convenient choice, but will still be much more cumbersome than a single stroller. Plan your outings accordingly.
- Minding twins at home or on outings is hard enough, but if you have other young children in addition to the twins, minding them and keeping them all safe becomes an impossible juggling act. Meticulous childproofing and strict rule enforcement are vital, and most public outings will require two adults. It's wise to prepare your older child or children for outings by explaining in advance how they must behave—for example, to hold onto the double stroller or shopping cart at all times.
- Even though with twins you have a built-in "buddy

A front-to-back stroller is safer and easier to handle than a double stroller with side-by-side seats.

system,'' it's a mistake to give them too much responsibility at too young an age. Many parents of twins develop a false sense of security from assuming that the twins will protect each other. Toddler and preschooler twins are just as vulnerable as toddler and preschooler singletons.

- Twins may collaborate ingeniously and egg each other on in making mischief. Be prepared for more trouble with climbing, exploring, escaping, breaking, and opening than you had with your singly born children.

Safety for Toddler Pedestrians

Parking lots:

Holding hands in parking lots should be a rule that you establish as soon as your child learns to walk and you should keep this rule in effect throughout the toddler years. If your toddler refuses to hold your hand, carry him or confine him to a stroller or shopping cart. If your hands are full, have the toddler hold onto your pocketbook strap, your sleeve, or belt loop. There are some situations in which you will have to let go of your toddler—for example, when you're opening the car door or unloading groceries or packages into the car trunk—and for these times you will need to devise certain rules and stick to them. One mother made it into a kind of game and told her toddlers to keep their hands on the car so that it wouldn't roll away. Another mother tries to keep herself between her toddler and the rest of the parking lot so he won't be able to get very far. Yet another mother keeps a close watch on her toddler when her hands are full and if he strays she says, "car" to remind him to stay put. If possible, try to strap your toddler into her car seat *before* you begin loading the groceries or whatever into the car to minimize the amount of time she is standing around without holding your hand.

Wanda, who lives in a rural area in Colorado where there is not much traffic, makes it a special point when she is in town to instruct her toddler son about the hazards of cars in parking lots: "When we're in a parking lot together, I get him to look for oncoming cars with me. I'm teaching him to recognize the difference between parked and moving cars." Other parents point out to their toddlers how invisible they are to drivers when they're standing between two parked cars. It's a good idea to explain repeatedly to your toddler how dangerous it is for him to dart out from between parked cars. Running in a parking lot—even in an open area—is a very serious offense indeed.

Sometimes we and our toddlers learn parking-lot lessons the hard way—by scares and near misses. My wife had a scare with our toddler daughter in a parking lot recently: she had let go of Emily's hand to get her car keys and at that moment a big truck rumbled down one parking-lot lane. Emily, who is extremely scared of loud noises, bolted in the opposite direction—and luckily there were no oncoming cars. Emily received a lecture about parking-lot safety and my wife made sure to keep her keys handier in the future. One mother said her toddler became much more cautious in parking lots after a near miss—but again, you cannot really count on a toddler to learn from experience. *You* must repeat the lessons, set down the rules, and enforce them.

Streets and driveways:

According to figures compiled by the National Safety Council, 1400 children under the age of five died in automobile accidents in 1989, and of this number 500 children died in pedestrian accidents. Toddlers are particularly liable to pedestrian accidents because they are small and thus difficult for motorists to see, they lack judgment about oncoming cars and yet they are very quick. *By far the most common toddler-pedestrian accident is running out into the street between parked cars.* Nearly half of the child-pedestrian accidents occur between 3:00 and 6:00 P.M. and many occur on Saturdays when parents are busy with chores, entertaining, and family routines.

Protecting your toddler from pedestrian accidents involves constant vigilance whenever your toddler is near the street. Unless your yard is securely fenced (see Chapter 3 for information on safe fences) you should *never* let your toddler play alone outside, even if you are keeping an eye on her from the window. When you are walking with your toddler on busy streets, insist on holding her hand or strapping her into her stroller. Make it a rule to walk—not run—on sidewalks, to stop at crosswalks, and to stop and wait before setting foot in any street, no matter how much or how little trafficked it is. Though traffic safety for a toddler is still entirely your responsibility, you can begin to teach your toddler to be a careful pedestrian by explaining rules and discussing traffic hazards and how to avoid them. Repeat the rule about stopping and looking both ways every time you cross the street.

The Automobile Association of America publishes a series of booklets for children on the subject of pedestrian safety. The titles in the AAA Early Childhood Traffic Education series include *When I Go Outside, I Listen and Look for Cars Coming, How I Cross a Street* and *Traffic Signs and Lights*. Contact the AAA, Falls Church, Virginia, 703–222–6000 to obtain copies. These important pointers were gathered from the AAA safety booklet for toddlers, from traffic safety experts, and from experienced parents:

- To prevent your toddler from running into the street, make it a habit to stop with your child before you cross the street and look both ways. Explain what you are doing—and do it each time you cross so the child will form the habit as well.
- Teach your toddler to identify oncoming cars, cars going away and cars backing up. Point out the backup lights that light up when cars are in reverse and listen for the high-pitched beeping sound that trucks make when they back up.
- Whenever there are cars—either parked or moving—keep your toddler within sight.
- Driveways are a particular hazard for toddlers because motorists backing out will not see a small child crossing the driveway. Thus you must teach your child to stop at driveways as well as streets, to look up toward the garage or house, and to stop if he sees a car backing out.
- Never call out to a toddler from one side of a street or driveway that he should cross over to you. Rather, tell the child to stay put and cross over yourself to get him.
- Set a good example of traffic safety when you are out walking with your toddler. Don't jaywalk, cross against the light, wander off the sidewalk, wade into lanes of

slow-moving traffic, or dart across busy intersections. You may think your child is too young to understand what you're doing, but you will be surprised at how adept and meticulous young ones are at imitating your behavior—both safe and unsafe.

A toddler is still much too young to cross a street or driveway unsupervised: these safety rules and precautions are really meant to build a sound foundation for the future. With a toddler, your safest bet is to expect him *not* to remember or obey the rules you have set. But if you lay a safe foundation now, you will have an easier time later on when your child does begin to walk to school alone or go out on short walks or errands by himself.

Tricycles:

The Consumer Product's Safety Commission reports that in 1989, some 9,600 children under five years of age suffered injuries in tricycle-related accidents serious enough to require treatment in a hospital emergency room. Though our toddlers love their first set of wheels, they must be protected from the hazards they involve. Most tricycle injuries occur because the child falls off, the tricycle tips over, the child gets his limbs entangled in the spokes of the wheel, he collides with something, or he is unable to stop the tricycle. A serious tricycle hazard is turning at high speeds: children have been flipped off their trikes when they attempt this. To keep your child safe on his tricycle, keep in mind these tips from the CPSC, from parents, and from safety authorities:

When you purchase a tricycle:

- Match the trike size with the child's size. A trike he has to grow into will be unsafe until he does; too small a trike will be unstable.
- Look for models that are low-slung, have widely spaced wheels, and are built with the seats close to the ground.

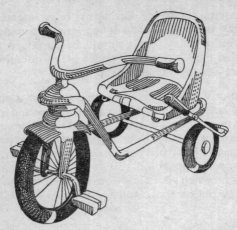

The safest tricycle is low slung with widely spaced wheels, a built-in seat close to the ground, and a brake.

- If possible, try to buy a tricycle with brakes and teach your child how to use them.
- Rough surfaces on handgrips and pedals will help your child keep his hands and feet in place and minimize falls and entanglements in wheel spokes.
- Don't buy a tricycle with protruding sharp edges or fenders.

When your child rides the tricycle:

- *Always supervise your toddler when he is riding in the street, near a driveway, or on a surface with even a gentle incline.* When you are supervising your toddler in the street, insist that he ride only on the side and repeat this instruction as often as necessary.
- A wide, smooth, unbusy sidewalk or a flat, hard-surface play area are the safest places for your toddler to ride his tricycle. Though grass will be a better cushion in

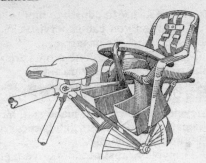

A safe child's seat for your bicycle.

case of a fall, the difficulty of getting traction on grass
and the unevenness of lawns make falls much more
likely.
• Instruct your child never to make sharp turns and never
  to ride downhill. Riding down steps and curbs should
  also be forbidden.

Biking With Your Toddler In Tow

If you enjoy biking yourself, you might want to equip
your bicycle with a safe child's seat with a strap so you
can take your toddler along for rides. If you do get such
a seat, you must also install a shield over the spokes of
the rear wheel to protect your child's legs from burns and
entanglement. *Your child must wear a properly constructed and properly fitted crash helmet whenever she
rides with you.* Remember always to strap the child into
the seat, to mount and dismount carefully when your child
is in the seat. It's more difficult to balance a bicycle when
you're carrying a passenger, so practice in empty parking
lots or quiet backroads before you head into traffic. You
may have to stress to your toddler the importance of
sitting quietly and not squirming around or continually
shifting her weight.

- If he likes to ride fast, try to convince him to limit his speeding to times when you can supervise closely and to safe places, such as parks or terraces.
- Never permit toddlers to ride double on a tricycle for this makes the tricycle extremely unstable.
- Teach your toddler to keep his hands and feet away from the wheel spokes.
- Check the tricycle periodically to make sure handgrips are in place, pedals and handlebars tightly secured, seats intact, wheels running smoothly.
- Never leave a tricycle to rust outdoors overnight.

Choosing and Instructing Baby-sitters

Chapter 2 covers the basics of choosing and training a baby-sitter for an infant, but as your child grows and changes some of the ground rules for the child's baby-sitter will change, too. You are fully aware of all the new places and things your busy toddler is getting into, but a baby-sitter may not be, especially if she hasn't been sitting for you on a regular basis. Review the basics of toddler safety with each new baby-sitter you use, and with old baby-sitters who haven't seen your child in some time. Point out cabinets and stairs that your child has attempted to raid or climb; if the child is still in a crib, remind the baby-sitter that she can climb out and so extra precautions must be taken to protect her from falls and to keep her from "escaping"; be sure to tell your baby-sitter to latch or lock inside doors to keep the toddler from getting out to the street.

Some very cautious parents prefer that the baby-sitters not give their children tub baths to avoid any possibility of drowning; instead they tell the sitter merely to sponge the toddler off before bedtime. In any case, children do not need to be bathed daily, aside from washing their hands and faces and brushing their teeth. If you have a pool, you may similarly want to keep the sitter and children away and out of any danger; if you are willing to permit the sitter to supervise your toddler in the pool, make very sure that the sitter is fully aware of water safety, particularly the importance of watching your child every moment he is in or near the water. Review your own pool rules with the sitter. Remind the sitter that a toddler can also drown in a toilet, a diaper pail, and a wading pool.

If necessary, make a list of all the new hazards your toddler is exposed to and go over each one carefully with the baby-sitter. Remember to tell the sitter that your children must never be left alone in the house, even for a moment, and that your toddler must never be left alone with your infant, even if the baby is in her carriage or playpen. Also review emergency procedures with the sitter and show her where you post emergency telephone numbers as well as the number where you can be reached. Instruct your sitter never to open the door to strangers.

One mother of a toddler son had a very good suggestion for parents who have a live-in care giver or who employ a sitter on a regular basis to mind their children during the day: sign up yourself and your sitter for a child safety course. Such courses, available through children's hospitals, adult education programs, local chapters of the Red Cross or YMCA, usually cover the basics of emergency first aid, CPR, pool and yard safety, and baby proofing. If it's difficult logistically for you and the sitter to attend together, take the course yourself first and then have your sitter attend the next session. Even the most careful and informed parents and care givers can learn a lot from such courses, and parents will feel that much safer knowing that their child's sitter has benefited from such a course.

(For information on choosing safe child care out of the home, see Chapter 7.)

6. Safe Habits and Attitudes

If babyhood is the period when your child makes the greatest leaps in motor development, toddlerhood is the period when your child is likely to make the most progress in his mastery of language. A one-year-old can understand a good deal of what you say and is even more adept at interpreting tone of voice; he can carry out some simple verbal commands; in all likelihood he says a number of words and may even string them together into short sentences. But by the time he reaches two or three, he can really carry on a conversation.* You can explain fairly complex concepts to him—for example, the difference between a stranger and a friend—and he can describe things he has seen (and imagined), what he feels and what he fears. This rapidly evolving mastery of language is the key to teaching a toddler safe habits and attitudes.

---

*Please note: not all children develop verbally at the same rate and a great many perfectly normal toddlers still have only the rudiments of language. The discussion here is based on *norms*, but remember that there are wide variations in what is considered normal.

A toddler's developing abilities with language are truly a marvel, but when it comes to safety you should keep in mind that even the most articulate toddler has certain fundamental limitations in comprehension and self-control. In many cases a toddler can *seem to* understand much more than he really does understand. Very often his verbal facility far outstrips his memory, his ability to learn from experience, or his capacity to apply what he has heard or even what he has said. A promise of obedience from a toddler is meaningless: to be on the safe side, expect him to forget and to disobey. However, keeping your expectations realistically low doesn't mean that you should pass up opportunities for discussion, explanation, and testing. If you put off instilling safe habits and attitudes until your child will obey and remember everything he has been told, it will be too late.

Safety Discussions: Getting Started

Chapter 2 introduced the idea of discussing safety with infants and early toddlers who are just beginning to understand and respond to language. Many of the concepts covered there still apply to a child in the toddler years:

- Safety is a subject that you will want to introduce often and at appropriate times when your child is willing and able to pay attention.
- It's best to make these discussions brief and to focus on one issue at a time. A toddler will become overwhelmed if you introduce too many rules and describe too many potential hazards at one time. A little at a time is best.
- Explain, don't lecture or issue orders when you are discussing safety matters with your toddler. Even hard-and-fast rules such as "Don't run into the street" or

"Don't touch the stove" should be accompanied by a brief, clear explanation of *why* this is a hard-and-fast rule.

• When discussing safety, get down on your toddler's level, both physically and psychologically. A game, song, or story will be easier to understand and remember than a monologue.

• Repetition is the key to making a child understand.

Once you have covered the basics of home, yard, and pool safety with your toddler, you are ready to move out to a wider sphere. One obvious guideline is to tailor your safety discussions to the situations and experiences your toddler commonly faces. If you live in a large city, you'll want to discuss correct behavior on sidewalks, crossing streets, buses, and subways; and you may begin to talk about how to deal with strangers. A suburban toddler will need to know about parking lots, streets, and driveways; shopping malls, pools, and playgrounds. The issue of strangers will come up for a child no matter where she lives. For tips on how to discuss each one of these issues, see below.

Another important guideline in discussing safety is to consider the maturity and basic personality of your child. Victoria said that her toddler sons "have no fear of anything—when they see a new person or new situation, off they go." These boys are clearly ready for discussions about strangers, personal privacy, and staying out of the road. So is Marge's toddler who, she says, "likes everyone" and is thus at risk of going off with a stranger. But Joan, who lives in the suburbs of New York, said her three-year-old daughter already has lots of fears, especially of strange men, and that discussing safety issues would only make her more afraid of the outside world. Joan plans to put off these discussions until her daughter has a little more self-confidence.

When I first mentioned to my toddler daughter that she could shout "*No!*" if someone touched her in a way she didn't like, she looked alarmed and confused. I thought I may have been jumping the gun with this issue, but a few days later she mentioned that one of the boys at her play school hugged her in a way she didn't like. I realized this subject would be easier for her to handle if I started by talking about what she could do when other *children* touched her; then, once she was comfortable with this concept, I could move on to the subject of strangers and adults.

There is a very delicate balance between preparing a child for some of the harsh realities of the world and preserving the beautiful, carefree innocence of childhood. As Jeri, the mother of three girls in Elkhart, Indiana, put it, "We want them to be prepared, and yet we wonder how to do it without scaring them to death." A toddler, no matter how physically or verbally adept, is still a very young child and should not be burdened with too many anxieties. If talking about safety upsets your toddler, if she's scared to go outside after you've mentioned the dangers of cars or strangers, or if her fantasies show that she's grappling with frightening issues that she really doesn't understand, it's time for you to back off.

Toddlerhood, particularly the period from two-and-a-half to three-and-a-half, is a time when fears mushroom in a child's imagination. Parents I spoke to said their toddlers were frightened by everything from the dark to water to sleeping in their beds to wearing socks indoors. Dogs, loud noises, unfamiliar people and places, imaginary monsters and witches are also common fears of this period. Dismissing a child's fears as nonsense is not fair to the child; it would be better to listen sympathetically, explain why the fears are unfounded, and reassure him. We may want to shelter a timid or fearful child a bit longer from some of the dangers and unpleasant facts of life. It would be better to wait until the child emerges from this very fearful stage and if necessary keep him out of potentially frightening encounters or situations.

Whenever you bring up the subject of safety, it's comforting for a child—even a very bold child—if you wrap-up your discussion on a positive note. "You can always tell me anything" and "I'll always be here to watch you and protect you" are sentences that can soothe a lot of the fears that safety issues may raise. A toddler who has grown accustomed to discussing safety matters in a low-key, nonthreatening way will be much more likely to be open with you later on if something *does* happen and less likely to assume the blame for the incident, as many children do.

How to Talk About Safety

Toddlers are not renowned for their long attention spans or for their ability to separate fact from fantasy. They are, however, intensely curious, enthusiastic about games, and many have amazingly good memories for songs and poems. When you discuss safety with your toddler, you have to take both their limitations and their special abilities into account. A toddler's distractability means that long, detailed lectures on safety topics are *out*. It's also probably a good idea to avoid too much buildup when you are introducing this subject. Informing a two-year-old that "we have to have a serious talk about your behavior in public" is likely to upset the child, if it doesn't bewilder him. Donnar, a Colorado mother of a three-year-old girl and a nineteen-month-old-boy, said that to keep from frightening her children about safety issues, she brings the subject up casually, as the need arises, for example when a car goes too fast in front of their house or when they're out shopping together and strangers talk to them: "I do not make it a formal, sit-down talk. Since I don't want the children to be scared, I try not to seem real worried when I talk about it." This is good advice. When safety discussions are part of everyday life, a child can absorb information gradually and is more likely to understand. Determining just how much a toddler does understand can be a bit tricky. Several parents reported that they brought up the subject of strangers, only to learn a few days later that their toddlers had no idea what a stranger was. Again, don't take too much for granted. Go slowly and keep the tone light.

One mother of a three-year-old said she always tried to weave safety messages into songs or games. "Every time we cross the street, we stop, we look both ways, we hold hands, and we sing. It's the same thing each time. The repetition really gets the idea across." Books are also a terrific way of introducing the subject. Creative Education in Mankato, Minnesota publishes a "Safety First" series of children's books with titles on bicycles, fire, home, outdoors, school, and water. *Dinosaurs, Beware!* by Marc Brown and Stephen Krensky (Little Brown and Company, 1982) is a humorous treatment of safety at home, outdoors, with animals, at the beach, in the car, etc. *Play It Safe* by Joan Webb (A Golden Book, 1986) covers safety situations from playground behavior to street crossing with bright clear pictures and easy-to-remember short poems. (Example: "Red means STOP, and Green means GO; A yellow light means Take it SLOW!") *The Berenstain Bears Learn About Strangers* by Stan and Jan Berenstain (Random House, 1985) teaches toddlers and preschoolers about strangers and the fears that children may develop. And Oralee Wachter's *No More Secrets For Me* (Little Brown, 1983) is a good introduction to personal privacy for slightly older children. Look for these titles and ask your local children's librarian for any other suggestions. Don't force these titles on your toddler. If he shows resistance to reading these books or if they upset him, look for other titles or introduce these subjects through stories or games that you have made up.

Many parents play "What if . . ." word games as a way of teaching toddlers (as well as older children) about safety. For example, you ask your toddler, "What would you do if you were playing in the park and your ball rolled into the street?" and see what she says. If her response is not the safe one, you tell her what *would* be safe and *why*. "What if . . . " games are a good way of finding out how much your child understands and what sort of discussions she is ready for. You can use these games to discuss just about any situation, from personal privacy to strangers, to fire safety to behaving in stores or on public transportation. When you first start playing "What if . . . " games, stick to the simplest situations. If your toddler doesn't seem ready or doesn't catch on, wait a few months.

What to Talk About

Strangers:

"One of my sons was out walking the other day and a lady in a car pulled over next to him. She said to him, 'I'm a friend of your mom's,' and she told him she'd drive him home. He hopped right in and off they went . . . "

Victoria was lucky: the lady really *was* her friend and she drove the six-year-old boy home—but it doesn't always turn out that way. Even though your toddler is too young to be out on the street or in a public place alone, it's still a good idea to begin teaching him how to deal with strangers.

When introducing this subject, first make it clear to your toddler that by "stranger" you mean *anyone* the child does not know. As Grace Hechinger points out in her book *How To Raise a Street Smart Child* (Facts on File, 1984), children often assume that by stranger you mean monster and that "a bad person will be easily identifiable" like a cartoon villain. This, of course, is not always the case. Many a child molester or abductor has come on with a smile, an offer of gifts or candy, a plea for sympathy, or a friendly seeming promise of some treat. Thus it's crucial to make your child understand that stranger means everyone—friendly or menacing, good or bad-looking—that she does not know.

Once your toddler understands what a stranger is, you can begin telling her how to act around strangers. All children should know that:

- They should not stop to talk to strangers in the street or yard.
- They can say *No* to any adult or any child.
- They should never accept rides or gifts from strangers; if a stranger offers these, the child should get away as quickly as possible.
- They should never approach a car when a stranger calls to them: rather, they should stay safely on the sidewalk; if the stranger in the car persists, the child should run in the opposite direction from the direction the car is going.
- If a stranger pursues them on the street, in a store, wherever, they should shout, run away, attract as much attention as they can.
- They do not have to be polite or helpful to adults.

Again, when discussing strangers with your toddler, take a gradual approach, don't cover all the rules at one time, and don't dwell too much on frightening situations. To lighten the tone, remind your toddler that *most* people are kind and that it's okay to be friendly when Mom and Dad are around. Carol, the mother of a four-year-old and toddler twins (all boys), said she has had some trouble drawing the distinction between acceptable and unacceptable public behavior for her kids: "When you have twins, strangers are always stopping you and asking 'Are they twins?' so it's hard to teach the kids not to talk with strangers. I just keep telling them that it's okay to smile but that you don't go off with people." I found that every time a stranger stopped to admire my toddler daughter, I'd instruct her to "say hi to the nice lady . . ." Later, when I started thinking about public safety, I realized I might be pushing her into bad habits. I've tried to explain to her, that it's okay to say "hi" to someone as long as she was with me or her mother, but if she doesn't want to, she doesn't have to.

Not all toddlers will be ready for discussions about strangers. If your toddler is very fearful, you might limit yourself to describing what a stranger is and to reassuring him that you would never let a stranger hurt him in any way. However, if you have one of those sunny, open, gregarious kids who tend to wander off and strike up conversations with everyone, it's time to begin talking about safety with strangers. In addition to the books and "What if . . ." games described above, you might want to act out little scenarios with your toddler. You play the stranger and get your toddler to shout "*No! Go Away! That's Not my Mother!*" The game may strike both of you as terribly funny, but it is good practice for your child in the event that he does face such a situation.

Personal Privacy:

A toddler has just as much right to personal privacy as you do, but much less control over it. How many parents have stood by and permitted overly demonstrative (or just plain intrusive) relatives, friends, and even strangers to touch and kiss their toddler in a way the child clearly did not like? It's socially awkward to tell another adult to back off, but we are really doing a disservice to our children if we don't interfere. The first lesson in personal privacy is one *we parents* should learn to follow ourselves: We should never permit our children to be handled in ways they do not like. If we allow our children's privacy to be invaded in our presence, we can hardly expect them to maintain that privacy when we're not around. Before we teach our children personal privacy, we must respect it.

An early toddler is probably still too young to understand the concept of personal privacy, but you can begin by teaching her the names of her body parts and by telling her that her body is her own. By the time they are pushing three, many toddlers are ready to understand that no one should touch them in the private parts or in ways they do not like. "We started discussing it with the girls (ages two and three) when they started school," said Marilu, a New Jersey mother. "My husband pointed to the private parts of their bodies and said, 'If someone touches you there, you say *No!* and come home and tell us.' Occasionally we would ask the girls after school if anyone had touched them there." Marilu's daughters showed no embarrassment over the subject and no reluctance to talk about it with their parents.

One way of defining personal privacy for a child is to say, "Everything your diaper covers is private" or "Everything your bikini covers is private." Again, as with all safety matters, try to be as specific as possible about what privacy means, what an unfriendly or abusive touch is, and what the child should do about it. Remember that in many cases the person invading the child's privacy is a relative or close friend of the family (of the reported cases of child molestation, strangers are responsible only one-third of the time; the other two-thirds of the cases involve neighbors, family friends, and relatives). This person may very well have tried to buy the child's silence. That's why it's so vital for you to reassure your child that she can tell you anything and that it's not her fault when someone abuses her. Many parents find that books are the most reassuring and least threatening way of bringing up this topic—see above for suggested titles.

The message you have taught your child in regard to strangers—*you can always say No to anyone*—applies to the area of personal privacy as well. Remember that the invasive act does not have to rank as a felony to be unpleasant and even frightening to your child. If your daughter doesn't like to be swept up and hugged by her uncle, or your son dislikes being tickled by the upstairs neighbor, then those acts should stop. Urge your child to say no by herself, but if that doesn't work, do what you can to put a stop to it. Telling someone "She doesn't like to be tickled" is usually all it takes.

For more about personal privacy and child sexual abuses, see Chapter 8. And for more about choosing safe day-care or preschool situations, see Chapter 7.

Safety At Home:

Childproofing is essential for keeping our toddlers safe at home, but childproofing alone is not enough, especially as the children get older and more adventurous. Chapter 3 covers the basics of childproofing for a baby and Chapter 5 includes a childproofing update for toddlers. In addition to these practical precautions, we can discuss home safety with our toddlers, so that eventually they will be able to recognize and avoid home hazards on their own. Little by little we may be able to relax some of our safety measures as our children gain knowledge and competence. For example, a stair gate is essential to keep a one-year-old out of danger; but most three-year-olds will be able to navigate stairs fairly well. If we take the time to demonstrate the use of banisters, to explain why it's important to be slow and careful on stairs, and why games on stairs are forbidden, we will probably be able to put away the gates.

As with all safety matters, *explanation* is the key to success in teaching a toddler about home safety. At some point your toddler will enter the "why" phase, demanding to know the reason for every conceivable phenomenon. This is an excellent opportunity to begin to explain *why* you have made certain home-safety rules.

Childproofing and child-resistant packaging account for the dramatic eighty-two percent decline in home poisonings for children under five in the past thirty years. We can make our toddlers even safer by explaining to them the difference between food and medicine, by repeating over and over that medicines are something to be taken

"Mr. Yuk" label tells your child the bottle is off-limits.

only when a parent gives it. Some toddlers may be old enough to understand the meaning of the "Mr. Yuk" label. If so, we should affix this label to all containers with hazardous contents and remind our toddlers frequently that containers so labeled are off-limits. Of course, such labeling should be done *in addition to* locking and storing such products safely out of reach.

For help with teaching toddlers and preschoolers about poisons, write to the Institute of Education Communications at the Children's Hospital of Pittsburgh, 1 Children's Place, 3705 Fifth Avenue at DeSoto Street, Pittsburgh, PA. 15213.

Though you would never leave a toddler unsupervised while the oven is on, or a fire is going in the fireplace or barbecue, you can explain while you're supervising your toddler why fire is something that we never touch.

Similarly safety in the bath, safety with toys, safety in the yard, and safety with younger siblings can all be the subjects of discussions and explanations. Let the setup and circumstances of your home determine the safety discussions you initiate with your toddler. By making such discussions a natural part of your everyday life, you're helping to instill safe habits and attitudes without arousing fears and worries.

Safety While Traveling and Visiting:

It makes good sense to take the time to prepare your toddler ahead of time when you take him visiting or traveling. The novelty of unfamiliar surroundings affects all children differently: some may become frightened, some will get very wild, others will determinedly explore every corner of another person's home or a motel room. Obviously you are going to have different safety concerns in these situations, and you can minimize the risks by discussing these concerns with your toddler before you make the trip. A suburban toddler who is venturing forth into the big city with his parents needs to be told about how to behave on subways and buses, how important it is to hold his parents' hands, on sidewalks and in stores. You will hold your toddler to higher standards of behavior in someone else's home than in your home, and some toddlers will obey if you explain this. We told our three-year-old that her grandparents' house was "very special" and that they would be very upset if she threw her food around, stood on the dining-room chairs, or played too wildly. This worked pretty well. Remember that you can't *rely* on safety discussions to keep your toddler out of mischief or danger in strange surroundings, but they may help and they will certainly set the right tone for the future.

One mother who has traveled frequently with her daughter had some good advice on the subject of taking little ones on trips: "We have traveled with our daughter since she was three weeks old, and each time we took her traveling it was a whole new experience since she was a different age. One rule we have maintained is that we don't take her out of her car seat to feed her. If she was screaming before we could stop, she screamed. Now that she's three, I can explain to her why I can't take her out or stop the car the instant she needs something. She accepts this." Another good tip about traveling with toddlers is to leave yourself plenty of extra time to stop on the road to let the little ones stretch their legs and burn off their excess energy. You might also describe to them ahead of time how long the trip will be, what forms of transportation it will involve and what new experiences they will come across. For example, if you're planning a plane trip, you might get a book about planes and airports, and then emphasize how important it is to stay close to you during baggage check-in, in busy public areas, and again when you're collecting your bags. This will reduce both the stress and the potential danger of traveling.

Toddlerhood is a funny, in-between age when your child is a kind of hybrid—part baby and part kid. In the course of a single day—or even a single hour—he will swing wildly back and forth from one to the other. There are times when he seems so mature, articulate, competent, and obedient that you can hardly believe he's only two; and other times when his behavior is much worse than an infant's—more willfull, more self-destructive, more dangerous, more heedless of the hazards all around. Keeping this complex and ever-changing individual safe is a real challenge that requires both mental and physical adroitness. As your toddler changes, you will be perpetually reevaluating your safety measures and rules. The eighteen-month-old who broke for the street the moment you turned your back will at age three very likely stand quietly by the car when you tell him to. The two-and-a-half-year-old may test every limit, break every rule, lie shamelessly about his transgressions, and then out of the blue announce that he's a big boy now and really act like one—at least some of the time. As the terribleness of the "terrible twos" wanes, your toddler will be much more likely to listen to reason and behave reasonably. At last after all those months of patiently explaining safety precautions, you feel like you're getting through to him.

Your toddler, in short, is graduating from toddlerhood and becoming a preschooler, by comparison a very responsible, law-abiding, considerate citizen. The baby that lingered on in the toddler years has vanished, but your preschooler, for all his bravado, eloquence, and self-confidence, is still a very young and very vulnerable child. Despite his newfound maturity, he's still, as you well know, a handful—and keeping him safe, at home, outdoors, and out in the world at his day care or nursery school, is still a demanding and consuming occupation. The next section of the book is your guide to safety during the preschool years.

Part Three

Testing the Waters: The Preschool Years, Ages Three to Five

7. Safety Away From Home

For many of our children the preschool years, ages three to five, will be the first time that they spend a significant part of their day away from home and in the care of adults other than their parents. Whether we send our preschoolers to an institutional day-care center, to a small informal play school run by a single caregiver, or to a family-home situation in which a mother looks after several young children in addition to her own, we obviously want the children to be just as safe as they are at home. Safety for preschoolers away from home means safe facilities and, even more important, responsible, trustworthy, and safety-conscious care givers. Finding a safe child-care facility and evaluating and monitoring the safety of the care givers who work there takes some effort and perseverance—but it is more than worth it for your child's well-being and your own peace of mind. The advice and suggestions in this chapter should make the effort considerably easier.

153

Choosing Safe Child Care

In out-of-the-home child care of any variety there are two fundamental safety considerations: the trustworthiness and reliability of the care givers and the quality of the physical setting. The only way you can evaluate both of these is by direct observation. Thus the first determining factor in deciding on day care is whether or not the facility or individual care giver permits visits by prospective parents and their children. If you are *not* permitted to go and inspect the facility and observe the care givers and children in action, cross that option off your list. One mother of two who takes in three preschoolers to her home said she not only permits visits from parents, she encourages unannounced drop-ins. That way parents can *really* see what is going on. When screening prospective day-care centers, try to visit the facility twice, once by yourself and once in the company of your child. Both of you should feel completely comfortable with the setting, the care givers, and the way the other children are behaving. If the place gives you or your child the "creeps," it is probably a good tip-off that something is wrong. "I let my four-year-old tour the preschool and talk with the other kids," one mother from a small town in Pennsylvania said. Afterward she asked him what he felt about the school. This way he felt he had some choice about attending.

In addition to personal observation, it's a good idea to inquire about the facility with state or local licensing agencies, with local child-care referral services, or the Better Business Bureau. Ask if there have been any past complaints and whether the center has consistently met with health and safety regulations.

In evaluating care givers, consider these points:

- Recommendations of other parents are your best guide outside of your own personal impressions. Ask the care givers for references, or better yet, talk with some of the parents at the end of the day when they are picking up their children.

- In observing care givers, pay particular attention to how they interact with children. Do they get down face-to-face on the kids' levels? Do they listen to and understand what the children say to them? Do the children seem to like and trust them? Do they seem relaxed around children? The way the care givers relate to the children is much more important than how well they relate to you.

- Researchers have identified a correlation between incidence of child sexual abuse and rigid discipline. Be certain to interview the director about the facility's discipline policy and observe how the staff members discipline the children. Does the stated policy accord with your own beliefs about discipline? Try to observe the reactions of the other children when a child is being disciplined. If they seem very frightened, it's an indication that the discipline is too severe.

- Ideally there should be two care givers for every twenty (or fewer) preschool children. A single care giver would have a very hard time minding ten or more preschoolers, so if you're considering a family-home situation with a single care giver, make sure the group is small.

- Trust your gut instincts.

- Ask the day-care director what sort of check they run on the backgrounds of care givers. What sort of staff turnover is there? If it is very high, you might want to avoid that center.

- If you are considering family-home day care, screen all members of the care giver's family who will come in contact with your child. Find out whether neighbors or older children drop by frequently when your child is at the home. If you feel that too many people have access to your child and that the care giver is too lax about this, consider using another family home.

- Good care givers will welcome, not resent, your concern about safety and appreciate your efforts to be involved. Evasive or abrupt answers to safety questions are a good tip-off that something could be wrong.
- Ideally care givers should be trained in CPR (cardiopulmonary resuscitation) and first aid. A large day-care center should have a nurse or doctor on staff.
- After enrolling your child in the day care, you may want to return periodically for visits to see how things are going, to observe new staff members, or just to check up (see "Monitoring day care" below).

In evaluating the physical facility, consider these points:

- Is the facility licensed? If so, this means it meets certain minimum standards of hygiene, fire safety, and health inspection. If not (for example, family-home day care is rarely licensed), you must check out these matters for yourself. Licensing alone does not mean the facility is safe, nor does the lack of a license in a family home or small, informal center or play school mean it is unsafe. You can run an extra check on licensed facilities by calling a state or local licensing agency or a child-care referral service to inquire about any violations or problems that other parents have reported.
- Where is the emergency exit located? Do you think the group of children could get to it quickly in case of fire?
- Does the room have adequate lighting and ventilation. Does the outdoor play area seem safe and reasonably clean? Are there many nooks and crannies where children are invisible to care-givers? Inspect playground equipment using the guidelines described in Chapter 5.
- If the child will be eating meals at the facility, you should

inspect the kitchen or food-preparation area closely for cleanliness. Do food preparers wash their hands before cooking and serving food? Are children also made to wash their hands before meals?

- Do the bathrooms seem clean? Are there a sufficient number of toilets and are they easily accessible to preschoolers?
- Are the stairways and any low windows closed off with safety gates?
- What sort of toys and arts-and-crafts supplies are in stock? Make sure paints and crayons are nontoxic, toys are safe, and that children cannot use the toys as weapons.
- What is the facility's policy in case of a child's illness? Is there any place where children with contagious infections can be isolated until their parents arrive? Obviously you do not want your child to be exposed to illness unnecessarily, though some exposure is unavoidable.
- How are emergencies handled? What sort of first-aid supplies are on hand?

Transportation to and from day care

Arranging for safe transportation to and from a daycare facility is your responsibility, but it is the responsibility of the care givers to see that the arrangements you have made for getting the child home are carried out correctly. It is essential that the care givers know about your transportation plans. If the plans are complex or constantly changing, give the care givers a written schedule at the start of each week. There are many stories about divorced or estranged parents without custody "kidnapping" their children from a school or day care center. The common ploy is for the estranged parent to claim that the legal parent has sent him or her to collect the child from school, or to intercept the child before he or she joins up with a car pool or gets on a bus. In order to prevent this—

or any other type of kidnapping—from happening, it is essential that you instruct the care givers *in writing* that they may not alter your specified transportation arrangements unless you authorize them either in person or in writing to do so. (For more about child abduction, see Chapter 11.)

If you are using some type of car-pool arrangement to get your child to and from her day care, also make some arrangement for the appropriate car seats or restraints for all the children—or at the very least, make sure that each child is safely belted in every time. You obviously don't want your child carpooling with a reckless driver, so try to find out about the driving habits and perhaps accident record of any new car-pool member. Three- or four-year-olds can make an awful lot of racket in the car, so you may have to make a special effort to concentrate on your driving and tune out distractions. Remember: safety comes first behind the wheel, and the children's insistent requests for more music, the retrieval of the apple or mitten that fell behind the seat, or whatever, can wait.

If the day-care center runs outings for the children, it is essential that you are told ahead of time what the outing is to be, how transportation will be arranged, and whether any extra staff members or parents will be involved in helping out. Volunteering to be such a helper (if you have the time) is a good way to keep tabs on what is going on at the center or school.

Monitoring your child's day care

As mentioned above, you will only want to enroll your child in a day-care facility or preschool at which *you* feel comfortable and welcome. If the care givers make a point of prohibiting visits by parents, you will be better off making other arrangements. When you place your child in a situation with a liberal and sensible visiting policy, make a point of dropping in periodically to see how things are going. For example, you might show up an hour before the time that you usually pick your child up, or simply stop by if you can spare the time. If the care givers are doing their jobs well and have nothing to hide, they certainly won't mind. It's also a good idea to develop a continuing relationship with your child's care givers. Discuss with them your child's adjustment and relationships with the other children; make them know how much you care; inform them of any new problems, fears, or unsafe habits your child has developed. One mother said she has become friends with the women who run her son's preschool and she often volunteers to accompany the group on field trips. Another mother has taken a volunteer job at her son's preschool. Of course, not all parents have the time or the ability to get *that* involved; but involvement needn't be at that level to be meaningful. It can be a matter of chatting with the care givers or center director now and then. A care giver who knows the parents and knows how concerned they are for their child's welfare is more likely to keep a close watch over the child and report any problems or potential problems as soon as they arise.

Sexual Abuse in Day-care Centers: The Facts

It is somewhat reassuring to know that sexual abuse of children in day-care centers is not nearly as widespread as a few highly publicized cases would lead one to believe. According to a 1988 report entitled "Sexual Abuse in Day Care: A National Study" led by David Finkelhor, Ph.D. and published by the Family Research Laboratory at the University of New Hampshire, there were an estimated 500 to 550 cases of "reported and substantiated" sexual abuse in America's 229,000 day-care centers from 1983 to 1985. The report calculates that for every 10,000 children enrolled in day-care centers (not including family-home day care), 5.5 children are sexually abused. As the report points out, this risk is "lower than the risk that children run of being sexually abused in their own households" (estimated at 8.9 per 10,000 children under six using figures from 1985).

Concerning the reported and substantiated abuse in day-care centers, the Finkelhor report reveals that:

• Men constituted 60% of the abusers even though they comprise only an estimated 5% of the staff of centers.
• The abuse occurs most frequently in the bathroom area.
• "Facilities with excellent reputations, well-qualified directors, and years of operation were just as likely to harbor individuals who sexually abused children."
• Abuse was less common in centers that parents could visit readily.

Children in day care, like children everywhere, run a risk of sexual abuse. But day-care centers are not the hotbeds of sexual abuse that the tabloids make them out to be. As the Finkelhor report concludes, "The risk of abuse is not sufficient reason to avoid day care in general or to justify parents' withdrawal from the labor force." Parents who send their children to day care (whether centers or family homes) should exercise the same caution about sexual abuse and prepare their children to avoid and report it in the same way that all parents do; there is, however, no need for them to be frantically worried or unduly suspicious.

If you do discover or suspect that your child is being sexually abused in his day care, notify the police and the local social service agency. Do not let the situation continue in the hopes that it will go away. Do not go to the school or center to voice your concern. Remember, you are not at fault for unfounded allegations of abuse as long as you make these allegations in good faith. If possible, contact other parents to find out whether they have detected any unusual symptoms in their children.

For more about preventing and detecting child sexual abuse, see Chapter 8.

Another very good way of monitoring what goes on at the day-care center or play school is to discuss it with your child. Ask your child regularly how his day went; what activities he engaged in; what other children he played with; how he feels about the care givers or teachers; what activities they organized; what they had to say to the children. You'll be amazed at how much comes out if you only ask. I discovered through one such conversation that my daughter's play-school teacher was giving the children gum, which I did not consider safe for three-year-olds. I was also informed that the teacher was lazy, silly, and had a couple of pet rabbits—none of which was the least bit true. So you may have to do some sifting of fact and fantasy. You probably know your child's various tones of voice and manners of expression well enough by now to distinguish between his tall tales and statements of fact.

If you hear something the least bit troublesome and the least bit plausible, pursue it with the care givers (except for instances of sexual abuse—see box—or physical abuse, which should be reported to the police). When discussing the day care with your child, try to avoid planting suggestions in his mind. Your leading questions and your child's unconsidered answers may conjure up a crisis where none exists in fact. If you have made a regular habit of discussing your child's day at day care with him in an easy, low-key way, you'll probably know right away when something out of the ordinary has happened. Remember that a matter need not be as dire as sexual or physical abuse to require your prompt attention and intervention.

Preparing Your Child for Safety Away from Home

Responsible care givers working at a safely constructed and well-equipped day care or home-care facility are not enough in themselves to keep your preschooler safe. Your child must be a cooperative partner where safety matters are concerned. This means she must be aware of safety, prepared for new situations she will encounter at pre-school or at a day-care center, and that she has been instructed on how to follow the directions given by care givers and how to get along with the other children. There is a fine line between drilling your child too hard to obey every command issued by an adult (dangerous if an adult wants to abuse your child) and giving your child too much license to disregard directions when she chooses. Obviously you want your child to obey when the care giver tells her to stop at the corner and wait before crossing the street, but you would want her to scream *"No! Leave me alone!"* if a care giver or any other adult or child tried to abuse her.

One way of handling this dilemma is to find out beforehand as much as you can about the routine that your child will be participating in at day care and then to go over each situation with your child before she begins attending. Explain to her that she must obey the teacher on all practical safety matters unless the teacher asks her to do something she *really* feels is wrong, for example, touching her in a way she doesn't like, telling her to lie, offering her gifts as bribes, threatening her with physical punishment, or actually using it. In those cases, she should first go to another teacher at school and then tell you about it as soon as she comes home. You should stress in all discussions that your child can *always* tell you *anything*. You might also want to play "What if . . ." games (see Chapter 6) based on likely events: "What if you were crossing the street at school and your buddy dropped your hand and ran ahead?" "What if the car pool driver didn't come and the other children said they were going to walk home?" "What would you do if the teacher insisted on coming into the toilet with you and looked at you or tried to touch you in a way you didn't like?" Once you have seen the facility and become acquainted with the activities, you will have a better sense of the "What if . . ." questions to ask. Remember when using this technique, explain *why* the correct answer is correct and ask only one or two questions at a time. You might also want to ask your local children's librarian for suggestions of books about starting school or going to day care. Some of these cover safety situations such as crossing streets in a group, playing considerately with toys, the importance of not pushing or shoving other children, sharing toys, etc.

If there are complaints about your child's behavior at preschool or day care, you should take the time to come in and if possible observe the situation for yourself, preferably without your child's knowledge (many schools have a one-way mirror). Discuss the problem with your child and if necessary with a trained counselor. A wild and uncontrollable child is a menace not only to her own safety but to that of her schoolmates as well. A care giver is obviously not going to be able to devote as much time to protecting this child from herself as you do at home. For your child's sake, take whatever steps are necessary to discipline her yourself and instruct her in safe, considerate behavior away from home. If you agree with the care givers' assessment of the situation and with the measures they are taking to correct it, make sure your child understands this. A parent who undermines a care giver (or vice versa) is only fanning the flames of the child's misbehavior. Care givers and parents should present a common front to children who need to be corrected and controlled for the sake of safety.

8. Child Sexual Abuse: Recognizing the Signs, Dealing With the Consequences, and Preventing It From Happening to Your Child

The Scope of the Problem

Sexual abuse of children is a problem that has come out of the closet in the past few years. It is not by any means a new problem, but it is a problem that has only recently begun to receive national attention. It is a problem that is surprisingly, even shockingly, widespread, and a problem that is on the rise in this country. According to statistics compiled by the American Humane Association, a non-profit organization concerned with the protection of children that was funded by the federal government to gather data about child abuse and neglect, there were 132,000 cases of child sexual abuse reported and substantiated in 1986 (the most recent year for which they have complete statistics). Other estimates run as high as 300,000. The comparable AHA figure for 1980 was 37,000 reported cases (part of the dramatic rise in reports stems from an increased awareness of child sexual abuse and an increased willingness to expose it). Although it is difficult to make estimates on the number of unreported cases, the Federal Bureau of Investigation puts the figure at five unreported cases for every case that is reported. We know from surveys of adolescents and adults about their childhood experience that incidence of sexual abuse is far, far higher than the reported cases (in a study of adult women conducted in 1983, 38% reported that they had been exposed to sexual abuse before the age of eighteen).

Sexual abuse of children need not involve intercourse to be considered abuse: it can be inappropriate fondling, an adult exposing himself to a child or forcing a child to expose him- or herself, or using the child for pornography or prostitution. Targets of sexual abuse are most likely to be older children—the average age of a sexually abused child is nine according to the American Humane Association, but 28.5% of abused victims are five or younger (other studies put the average age as low as 8.5 and as high as 13). According to a 1987 study of 403 child molesters conducted by Dr. Gene Abel, boys are even more likely to be abused than girls. Clearly this is an issue that every parent and every child must be aware of.

Who Are the Abusers?

One of the most disturbing facts about child sexual abuse is that in the overwhelming majority of cases the abuser is someone the child knows, trusts, even loves. American Humane Association figures indicate that in 1986 (the most recent year for which such statistics are available) 42% of the reported cases of child sexual abuse involved the child's parents (including step parents and adoptive parents) and 22.8% were perpetrated by other relatives. This means that only one-third of the reported cases are outside the family, although, as AHA information specialist Katie Bond points out, the abusers counted as outside the family may be the boyfriend or girlfriend of the child's parent. In about 77% of the cases reported in 1985, the abusers were male.

Abusers outside the family circle are likely to be men who have placed themselves in positions in which they are frequently alone with and responsible for children. They might be scout leaders, youth ministers, Big Brothers, day-care workers, schoolteachers, favorite neighbors. They are the men about whom everyone says, "Oh, he's great with kids. Kids love him." In most cases they seem perfectly normal, and they are likely to be married and have children of their own. Abusers who prey on boys are unlikely to be homosexual in their adult sexual contacts. One physician who studies child abusers points out that none of the men he has treated fits the stereotype of the creepy pervert who goes around in a raincoat and carries candy in his pocket. Nor are they "dirty old men": a study by a former executive director of the American Humane Association shows that the median age of the sex offender is thirty-one. In a pamphlet published by the National Committee for Prevention of Child Abuse (see resource section at the end of this chapter), Cornelia Spelman lists a number of signs that *may* help identify abusers, including: heavy alcohol and drug use; having been abused themselves as children; wife battering; social isolation; extreme overprotection of their own children; a tendency to treat children as property and show no respect for their privacy; a tendency to make sexual comments about a child's appearance.

The abuse of a child is unlikely to be a one-time event. In the typical case the abuser "stalks" the child over a period of time, playing on her trust and affection in the case of family members or, if the abuser is outside the family, winning her affection by giving her gifts or special attention. Once the abuse begins, he will enforce her silence through threats. He might threaten to kill her or one of her parents if she tells anyone about what they have been doing. He will make the child believe that she is to blame. The longer the abuse continues, the more difficult it becomes for the child to stop it or to seek help. Abusers usually have a large number of victims and may prey on hundreds of children before they are found out.

Parents who discover that their children are being sexually abused face one of the most difficult crises of parenthood. It is a crisis that must be handled swiftly, but delicately—and above all in such a way as to spare inflicting any more pain on the abused child. How do you know if your child is being abused? How do you discuss the situation with him without deepening his trauma? How do you put a stop to the abuse? What legal action should you take against the abuser? If the case goes to court, what impact is it likely to have on your child? Parents who discover (or suspect) that their child is being sexually abused need answers to these questions. This chapter contains these answers as well as advice on keeping your child safe from abuse and a list of resources for further help.

The Signs of Sexual Abuse

Since child abusers go to such lengths to disguise their acts and to buy the silence of their victims, it is often very difficult to discover the situation. In the rare event that your child comes right out and tells you she is being abused or drops hints in a vague way about some trouble she is having with an adult, believe what she is saying and follow up until you determine the exact nature of her complaint. *It is very uncommon for a child to lie about sexual abuse or to invent stories about it*. You may find your child's allegations incredible at first, but do not make the mistake of dismissing them. Be alert to veiled statements such as "he was fooling around with me" or "he does things to me" or "I don't like it when we're alone." These may be your child's way of telling you that she is being sexually abused.

It's much more common, however, for a sexually abused child to say nothing about the situation. The child may be too ashamed of what is happening to speak up, or the abuser may have threatened her in some way, either scaring or bribing her into silence. Many children feel they somehow *deserve* the abuse or they worry that their parents won't love them anymore if they find out what has been happening. In other cases a child may simply lack the power of expression to describe what has been happening, or the child may have told you in ways that you did not understand or chose not to understand. In all of these cases, the only sign of the sexual abuse will be some change in your child's behavior or appearance. Keep an eye out for these warning signs of sexual abuse:

- depression, mood swings, outbursts of temper or aggression
- difficulty concentrating
- unusual quietness and docility
- sleep disorders
- bedwetting
- weight loss
- unusual fearfulness toward adults, avoidance of touch from family members or friends
- unusual fears associated with specific places, such as bathrooms or showers
- signs of distress or fear when clothes or diapers are changed; signs of shame about his or her body
- fear of playing alone
- unusual or sudden interest in sexual topics or curiosity about particular sexual practices; inappropriate displays of sexual behavior at home or sexual play with friends

- any unusual appearance in or discharge from the child's penis, vagina, or anus, including itching, bleeding, swelling, rawness, complaints of pain
- noticeable straining when the child sits down or walks

If your child shows some or many of these warning signs over a period of time, it is essential that you take action. Try to determine who could be abusing your child; take a hard look at your child's day hour by hour to see if there are any blocks of time when he comes in contact with an adult who might be abusing him; sit down and talk with your child about your fears and suspicions.

Discussing the Situation with Your Child

If your child informs you that he has been sexually abused or if you discover it through some other means, the first thing you want to do is to reassure the child that *you* still love him. Sexually abused children are living with so much fear and shame that if you display hysteria or anger when you find out about the situation, you may be adding to your child's fear. No matter how shocked and furious you are about the situation, try to vent your emotions and calm yourself down *before* you discuss the subject with your child. No matter how traumatized and violated *you* feel, your child feels that much *more* violated—even if he can't express it or show it.

Your role is to comfort and reassure your child, to find out what you can about the situation, and to make your child believe that you are behind him all the way. Let him know how sorry you are for what happened and how proud you are that he can talk about it with you. Keep in mind that many abused children blame themselves: the last thing you want to do is make your child feel criticized or guilty for having told you or for having been discovered. In child-sexual-abuse cases the adult is *always* to blame for initiating and continuing the abuse, *never* the child. Remember to let your child know that he has done no wrong. And remember this yourself. It's not uncommon for parents of sexually abused children to feel that their children have lost their innocence and are now irreparably "damaged goods." The children very often feel this themselves. Even if you feel this in your heart, it's essential not to communicate it to a child, but to treat the child with as much love and respect as you did before you discovered the abuse. Be sensitive in your questions and comments to the fact that the abuser may be someone the child loves and trusts.

If possible, let your child take the lead in discussing the situation, in revealing his feelings, and in describing what happened. If you barrage your child with questions, you may confuse him or cause him to hide some crucial information. In many cases a child may have complex feelings toward the adult who was abusing her: this person may have a strong emotional hold over your child and may have bought her love (or won her love) before the abuse began. For you to come out and say, "He deserves to go to prison for what he did to you!" may only upset your child further. Make it clear that you think the abuse is wrong, but avoid leading questions along the lines of "Didn't you know you weren't supposed to be doing those things?" that make your child feel responsible. Also avoid questions beginning with *why?*, for example "Why didn't you tell anyone?" or "Why didn't you say no?" Whenever possible, be supportive of your child and positive about her own role in the situation; let her know that you think she's very brave for talking with you about this.

You should be the first to discuss sexual abuse with your child, and you should be willing and open to discuss the situation as often as your child needs to. But no matter how consoling and understanding you are, your child will very likely still require some sort of psychological counseling to help him through the situation. Even if the abuse consisted only of an isolated incident and involved only fondling or exhibitionism, your child may have been seriously traumatized. "Counseling is absolutely crucial even if the child is not displaying any symptoms," according to Jan Kirby-Gell, sexual-abuse specialist at the National Center on Child Abuse and Neglect. "Without some sort of counseling the children really don't get over it." In some cases the full extent of the trauma emerges only after the abuse comes to light. Your child may feel judged and condemned by you or by society; he may feel he is not as good as other children anymore; or his trust in adults, including his own parents, may be severely shaken. For all of these reasons, outside counseling may be critical to your child's recovery. Keep in mind, however, that outside counseling does not mean that you should never discuss the situation with your child again. Your continuing support, affection, and openness can only be to your child's benefit. Even with outside counseling and support from loving parents, a child may show the signs of trauma for a long time after being sexually abused. Nightmares, new fears, including a fear of going outside, and reversion to infantile behavior are common aftereffects of sexual abuse. These symptoms may get worse after the abuse has been exposed and then, once the child is able to regain his trust in adults and in the world around him, gradually fade.

Kirby-Gell of the National Center on Child Abuse and Neglect advises parents to seek out counseling "aggressively" and to look for counselors who have experience with abused children. Experienced counselors can be found through rape-crisis centers, mental-health facilities, social-service agencies, local chapters of Parents United and Parents Anonymous, your child's pediatrician, or the National Organization for Victim's Assistance in Washington, D.C., 202–232–6682.

Counseling also can be of use to you in dealing with the distress and rage you feel about the abuse. Just as you don't want your child to blame herself for the abuse, so you should try not to blame yourself for what you might have or should have done. Counseling or conversations with a social worker who has experience with abused children may also be useful in instructing you how best to discuss the situation with your child. In addition, counseling can be a first step toward helping custodial parents deal with the growing problem of false accusations of abuse made by estranged parents.

When sexual abuse occurs within the family, as it does in about three-quarters of the reported cases, Kirby-Gell advises that the entire family should enter some sort of therapy.

Taking Action

A sexually abused child requires a thorough medical examination. In the unlikely event that your child informs you of sexual abuse involving physical violation on the same day that it occurs, do not wash the child or his clothing until after the exam. Carefully preserve whatever evidence you can. A prompt medical examination is a must even if you learn of the abuse long after it has happened. If you feel that your family doctor is not qualified to examine a child for sexual abuse, contact the local Office of Protective Services or the local chapter of the American Academy of Pediatrics for help in finding a doctor who is specifically trained to diagnose child sexual abuse.

Child sexual abuse is a crime, and if you know or suspect someone is committing this crime, you should report it to the police and to your state's department of social services (this may also be called the department of human services, youth services, family services, or social or public welfare, depending on the state—the number will be included with the state government listings in your phone book). In some states both a police detective and a social worker will be assigned to investigate the case. Reporting an incident to a state department of social services is especially important because a social worker can provide counseling to you and your child, or assist you in finding a good counselor who has experience in this area.

It is natural for any parent to want to seek revenge if his or her child has been abused, but the decision about whether or not to press for the prosecution of a sexual abuser is not always as simple as it may at first appear. The trial process can be extremely traumatic both for you and your child. Patricia Toth, director of the National Center for the Prosecution of Child Abuse in Alexandria, Virginia, offers this general picture of the court process and how it affects the child victim (the specifics vary from state to state and case to case):

"Once the case is reported, there is an investigation interview with the child conducted by a police officer and/or social service worker. Hopefully they will coordinate and not have to repeat the interview. Since it is often hard for the child to talk about what has happened, it may take several interviews for the child to disclose everything. The local authorities try to have the same person talk with the child each time.

"Once the child has been interviewed, other witnesses are interviewed, evidence is gathered, and the police transfer their records to the prosecutor's office. Some states have a grand jury to determine whether to indict, and in some states the child will testify at the grand jury trial, although there will be no cross-examination by the defense. In other states there is a preliminary hearing to determine probable cause, and here the child is more likely to be cross-examined by the defense attorney.

"Assuming that after this the case is still alive, a trial date is set and the child will be prepared for a court hearing. A victim advocate will familiarize the child with the court setting, showing him or her an empty courthouse and letting the child sit in the witness stand.

This helps make it as unscary as possible. Right before the trial, it's very common for children five and under to have a competency hearing at which the judge determines whether the child understands the obligation to tell the truth and whether the child has the memory and verbal ability to testify in court.

"At the trial itself the child has a direct examination by the prosecutor and a cross-examination by the defense attorney. Every effort is made to make the child as comfortable as possible. It's quite rare for a child to be attacked by a defense attorney—that is really not a smart move in front of a jury. By and large, that happens only in the movies."

Toth adds that in most cases parents are requested not to discuss the abuse with the child prior to the trial so that the child doesn't seem to be rehearsed or to be reciting a script written by the parents. "It makes for a stronger case if the child is spontaneous and natural," she says. To this end, the parents are very often asked to leave the courtroom during the child's testimony so that the child will not turn to them for prompting.

At the end of the trial if there is a conviction, there will be a sentencing hearing and in some cases the judge will call upon and consult with the child at this time. Having some input in the sentencing process may help restore a child's self-esteem. Toth says that although sentences vary tremendously depending on the severity of the case, there is a fairly good chance in the less serious cases that an offender with no prior record will qualify for a suspended sentence and enter some sort of treatment program. Toth estimates that fewer than 5% of the reported cases of child sexual abuse result in prosecution, but that for cases that are prosecuted, the conviction rates are fairly high.

Even though prosecutors do what they can to shield children from stress during sexual-abuse trials, the court process may be a very rough time. If you have not already sought out psychological counseling for your child, you will want to do so during the trial. You should also take whatever action you can to protect your child during the court process. Try to have his testimony videotaped so that he does not have to repeat it; discuss the case in detail with the prosecuting lawyers so you can reassure your child about the events he will be facing in court. Tell your child often that you love him and are proud of him for speaking up in court; let him know that *you* understand he is telling the truth, even if the defense attorney tries to make it appear that he is not.

Even if the case is not prosecuted, you must take whatever steps are necessary to see that the abuse stops at once and that it will not start again. Within the family this will probably mean confronting the abuser, getting him psychological help, and separating him from the abused child.

Keeping Your Child Safe from Sexual Abuse

There is no way to guarantee that our children will never be sexually abused, but there are a number of practical, workable ways that we can diminish their risk and help them put a stop to the situation rapidly if it does occur. At the heart of almost all of these prevention techniques is a strong bond of love and open and free communication between parent and child. Abusers commonly prey on the most vulnerable children—unloved, neglected children who are most likely to respond to their special attentions and fearful, timid children whom they can most easily silence through threats. Other factors that have been associated with children who are at greater risk of sexual abuse include: the presence of a stepfather; the child's having lived apart from his mother or having a poor relationship with her; the child's having few if any friends. Also, children who were abused once are at serious risk of being abused again. Self-confidence, good social adjustment, and close, loving relationships with both parents provide a child an important barrier against abuse. If your child feels that he can come to you to discuss any issue or event in his life and if he feels confident enough of himself and of his relationship with you that he can project that confidence out to the world at large, he is already several big jumps ahead of the typical sexual-abuse victim.

When discussing sexual abuse and the methods for preventing it with your child, use the same approach you use in talking about other common safety issues: bring the subject up informally or when it arises on a television show or book, and talk about it briefly in a low-key way. Don't make a big deal about these discussions or give them a lot of buildup. One good way to begin teaching your child to protect herself from sexual abuse is to instill in her a good sense of personal privacy. (For more on discussing personal privacy as well as other safety matters with young children, see Chapter 6.) Teach her the correct names for all her body parts, including the private parts, from an early age and let her know that her body belongs to her and her alone. If she doesn't want someone to touch her in a certain way—even if it's a kiss from grandma or a hug from a favorite uncle—that is her right, and you should support her. Coercing a child to accept unwanted physical contact leaves her less equipped to ward off the advances of a child molester.

A preschooler is old enough to understand the difference between good and bad touch (bad touch makes you feel bad inside—similar to the way you feel when a favorite toy gets lost) and also that her private parts—the parts covered by a bathing suit—are not to be touched by anyone else. Be specific in your discussions of personal privacy: saying something like "No one except your doctor should ever touch your vagina" will make a clearer impression on a child than saying "The parts *down there* are private." You may feel embarrassed about saying penis, vagina, or anus to your children, but your children will not be embarrassed about hearing or repeating these words. If necessary, practice by yourself, with your spouse, or in front of a mirror until you can discuss the topic without feeling uncomfortable. If you talk about personal privacy in the same matter-of-fact way that you talk about other safety issues, whatever embarrassment you feel will soon vanish. Introduce the subject when it comes up naturally—in the bath, for example.

Once you've helped your child establish a strong sense of personal privacy, you can begin to introduce the subject of sexual abuse and how your child should respond if she ever encounters it. In all such discussions, it's best to go very slowly, to stress the positive, to be specific without being alarmist, to make sure you are getting the message across. "I started talking about the subject with my kids when they were two and I did it in little pieces so that they're not traumatized," said Heidi, the mother of a seven-year-old girl and a five-year-old boy. "We discuss it little by little. I have a friend who sat her daughter down the day before kindergarten started and dumped the whole thing on her then. It really scared the girl!" Marge, who was sexually abused herself as a child, is careful not to communicate her nervousness about the topic to her daughter: "We talk about it when something comes up on TV or with books. I want her to be cautious, but I don't want to overdo it."

Heidi also emphasizes to her children that they should trust their feelings: "I tell them, if someone does something that doesn't feel right to you, then it's wrong. Your feelings are always right." Jan Kirby-Gell of the National Center on Child Abuse and Neglect points out that most children have a strong intuitive sense of right and wrong: they know when something makes them feel "funny" or "creepy." This intuitive sense can be a good basis on which to build up your child's awareness of personal privacy.

All children should be taught the three things to do if anyone tries to touch them in a way they don't like:

1. Say *no!*
2. Run away.
3. Tell their parents what has happened.

In teaching these rules to preschoolers, you can invent games, skits, rhymes, or whatever other kind of creative activity your child seems to enjoy. Kids this age love to act, shout, and throw their weight around—and acting out the correct response to a child abuser can be a good opportunity for them to do all of these things. "What if . . . " word games can also be an effective way of reinforcing the message and determining how much your child understands. After you've discussed the three rules, you might ask something like, "What if someone at your nursery school told you to come in the bathroom with him and pull your pants down?" The correct response would be the three rules or some variation on them. If your child comes out with a totally inappropriate answer, it's a signal to go back to basics with her.

As your child gets older and spends more of his time away from home, you will want to focus your discussions of sexual abuse on the specific dangers that he might encounter. In a low-key, nondramatic fashion, you might explain that although most people are good-natured and kind to children, there are some sick individuals who take advantage of children. Explain in some detail what these people might attempt: touching him in a way he doesn't like, making him take off his clothes, making him touch them. If you merely say, "There are sick people who molest children," your child will either have no idea what you're talking about or will use his imagination to fill in the picture in a very frightening way. Stress that these people are the exceptions. And stress that your child can keep himself safe from them by saying no, getting away, and telling you. You might set up a few examples of what a child molester might try and how your child should respond, for example:

> "If someone—even someone you know—tells you to sit on his lap and you don't want to, say 'No, I won't do that.' "
>
> "If someone in the park takes down his zipper in front of you, you can run away and tell me."
>
> "If someone you know tries to make you keep a secret about something that makes you feel funny, come and tell me about it—even if he said you shouldn't, even if you promised you wouldn't."

Child abusers will always coerce and threaten their victims into keeping the abuse a secret; if you can explain to your child the difference between *good* secrets that are okay to keep (for example, a surprise party or a birthday present) and *bad* secrets that he should *never* keep (any secret that another adult tells him to keep from you), you've made a big step toward protecting him from prolonged abuse. Younger children probably won't get this distinction, and you can just tell them never to keep *any* secrets from you. Reassure children that nothing bad will happen to them if they tell secrets.

Another very good way of bringing up sexual abuse and personal privacy is to read a book on the subject together. Titles on the subject appropriate for preschoolers include *No More Secrets For Me* by Oralee Wachter (Little Brown, 1983), four stories about kids facing sexual abuse; *It's OK To Say No* by Amy C. Bahr (Grosset-Dunlap, 1986), a coloring book for two-to-six-year-olds that brings out the message that kids can say no to adults; *A Better Safe Than Sorry Book* by Sol and Judith Gordon (Ed-U Press, 1984), a book that conveys the message to get away from threatening situations and to tell parents about bad things; *I Belong to Me* by Barbara Pawson and Linda Kemp Keller (Whortleberry Books, 1984), in which two children talk about unwanted touching; *I Can Say No* by Shirley Seltz (Seltz Associates, 1985), which reassures kids that they can say no even to adults they love; *It's MY Body* by Lory Freeman (Parenting Press, 1984), which instructs kids about the different kinds of touch, from tickling to sexual abuse; *My Body is Private* by Linda Walvoord Girard (Albert Whitman & Co., 1984), in which a girl describes how she gained a sense of personal privacy; *Trust Your Feelings* (C.A.R.E. Productions Association of British Columbia, 1984), which treats sexual abuse in a nonthreatening way; *A Very Touching Book* by Jan Hindman (McClure-Hindman Books, 1983), a book that tells kids how to recognize different kinds of touch; *Private Zone* by Frances Dayee (Charles Franklin Press, 1983), which encourages kids to discuss personal privacy with their parents; *What If I Say No!* by Jill Haddad and Lloyd Martin (M.H. Cap and Co., 1982), a workbook for kids that includes "what if" situations, and for older children *Feeling Safe Feeling Strong* by Susan Neiburg and Janice E. Rench (Lerner Publication, 1984), a series of stories about child abuse.

In addition, there are a number of good videotapes for children on the subject, including "Strong Kids, Safe Kids" hosted by Henry Winkler (Paramount Video production); "Child Sexual Abuse: What Your Children Should Know" (Indiana University Audio-Visual Center); "Better Safe Than Sorry II" (FilmFair Communications); "Feeling Yes, Feeling No" (Perennial Education); "Now I Can Tell You My Secret" (Walt Disney Educational Media Co.).

Good books on the subject intended for parents are *Your Children Should Know* by Flora Colao and Tamar Hosansky (Bobbs-Merrill, 1983), which helps parents devise a self-protection program for their kids and teach them safety without making them fearful; *The Safe Child*

Book by Sherryll Kerns Kraizer (Delacorte, 1985), which covers safety for kids staying alone, safety in day care, and how to teach kids about safety without overloading them with anxiety; *The Silent Children: A Parent's Guide to the Prevention of Child Sexual Abuse* by Linda Sanford (McGraw Hill, 1980), which discusses a number of family safety techniques; and for more detailed information on facts of child abuse, *The Source Book on Child Sexual Abuse* by David Finkelhor (Sage Publishers, 1986).

Sexual-Abuse Resources

National Committee for Prevention of Child Abuse
332 South Michigan Avenue, Suite 1600
Chicago, IL 60604–4357
312–663–3520
An organization dedicated to preventing child abuse through advocacy, education, and research. Provides a variety of publications on the subject as well as listings of sixty-seven local chapters. Contact them for a free list of publications and educational materials.

Clearinghouse on Child Abuse and Neglect Information and the Clearinghouse on Family Violence Information
P.O. Box 1182
Washington, D.C. 20013
703–821–2086
Provides extensive bibliographies on the topic of child abuse, including sexual abuse.

800–4–A–CHILD
A twenty-four hour hotline sponsored by Childhelp USA; refers callers to counselors and support groups through local chapters of Parents Anonymous and Parents

United (see below); provides assistance to callers in finding the proper channels to report incidences of child abuse. Many local chapters of Parents Anonymous offer counseling to parents who are abusing their children or to the spouses of abusive parents.

Parents United/Daughters and Sons United
P.O. Box 952
San Jose, CA 95108
408–453–7616

National organization with local groups that provide assistance to families involved in child sexual abuse, for parents who were sexually abused as children and, through Daughters and Sons United, to children who are victims of sexual abuse.

C. Henry Kempe National Center for the Prevention and Treatment of Child Abuse and Neglect
1205 Oneida St.
Denver, Colorado 80220
303–321–3963

A clinically based resource for research, consultation, and program development in the area of child abuse. Offers a wide range of publications for sale to the general public.

National Organization for Victim's Assistance
1757 Park Road, NW
Washington, D.C. 20010
202–232–6682

Assists in therapeutic referrals for victims of child abuse; upon request will mail information packets on the subject of child sexual abuse.

9. Keeping Pace With Your Growing Child

The preschool years, ages three to five, are a wonderful time for parents and children. A preschooler can do so many things, go so many places, understand so much, and communicate so well. And she can do so much more by and for herself than she could as a toddler. She is likely to disappear into her room for long stretches of independent play or play unattended with a friend or sibling. When you are out in the park or the yard with her, you don't need to hover the way you did with an infant or toddler. The equipment needed to transport, feed, and entertain a preschooler safely is far simpler and far less cumbersome than the safety equipment that babies and toddlers require. Your preschooler can probably out-climb, outrun, outtalk, and outsmart *you*. She is agile, dexterous, creative, quick-witted, curious, determined, persistent, cooperative (when she feels like it), rebellious (usually when it's least convenient for you), inventive (in both games and mischief), explorative, insistent on finding out the reason for every occurrence she comes across or

183

hears about, and she has an excellent memory (for certain things). She thinks her powers of mind and body are limitless, until she collapses in the deep, peaceful sleep of childhood.

Keeping this bundle of physical and mental energy safe involves new challenges as well as welcome relief from some of the vigilance you had to exercise a few years back. Since your preschooler moves in a wider world than she did as a toddler, she is exposed to more potential hazards, but she also has more judgment and better physical coordination to help keep her safe. As she struts around the playground, sits demurely in restaurants, dresses and washes herself, helps you cook or take care of a baby, she seems very grown-up indeed; but right beneath all that newfound bravado, expertise, and maturity, she is still a young child who needs not only your love but your protection. The love comes naturally; the protection is the subject of this chapter.

Is Your Preschooler Ready Yet? An Activity Checklist

Because a preschooler's behavior is so complex and so changeable, it's sometimes difficult to know when the child is ready to be trusted on his own with certain activities. The checklist below is a guide to some of the activities that the *average* preschooler is and is not ready for. Of course every child is different and matures at a different rate, so do take your own preschooler's needs and abilities into account when consulting the checklist. In general, the age estimates here are on the conservative side. If you feel your child is ready to be trusted with some new activity, start slowly and stay nearby for the first few times.

Can a preschooler be trusted alone in the bathtub?

No. Even if your preschooler can swim fairly well, you wouldn't trust him alone in a swimming pool—and the same caution applies to the bath. A child can drown in a bathtub full of water just as easily as he can drown in a pool. So don't neglect your duties as bath "lifeguard."

Can a preschooler be trusted on the stairs?

Yes. Most preschoolers can go up and down the stairs by themselves without needing adult supervision. However, it is essential to stress that stairs are *not* a place for wild games, for jumping, throwing things, or pushing. It is also essential that you keep your stairs clear of all clutter. Encourage your child to hold onto the banister when using the stairs.

Can a Preschooler Ride in a Car with Just a Safety Belt?

Maybe—but it's safer to continue using some type of car seat or harness. Since a child is safer in a safety seat, keep him in it until he outgrows it, which for most seats is between forty and sixty pounds. Then, the safest course is to graduate him from his toddler car seat to a car booster seat with a harness (see Chapter 11); in the event of a crash or sudden stop, the seat will absorb some of the belt's impact and thus protect your child from possible internal injuries. Most models can be used until the child reaches eighty pounds. Remember, once you've put the car seats away, you *must* strap your child in with a seat belt, preferably a shoulder belt. "The car doesn't start unless their seat belts are buckled" is a rule a mother of a seven-year-old girl and a five-year-old boy has laid down. No matter what age your child is, he or she is safest in the middle of the car's backseat and least safe in the front seat next to the driver. If you're using a car pool to get him to preschool, make sure the other drivers also use seat belts for all the children.

Can a Preschooler Be Trusted to Cross the Street Alone?

No. A preschooler lacks the judgment and memory to cross the street without adult supervision. Continue to repeat safety instructions—stop, look both ways, never go in the street alone—each time you cross the street with your preschooler. He is old enough to learn the difference between road, curb, and sidewalk, and some children this age can be trusted to stay on the sidewalk or on the safe side of the curb without holding your hand or staying by your side all the time.

Can a Preschooler Memorize His Address and Phone Number?

Maybe. Individual variation is tremendous. You should keep reminding your preschooler about this crucial information, and in discussions about how to act if he ever gets lost or separated, remind him that he should only repeat this to a police officer or security guard. You might reinforce the message with "What if . . . " games: "What would you do if you got lost at the museum?" "What would you say if a police officer with a blue uniform asked you, 'What's your name little boy? Where do you live?' "

Can a Preschooler Be Trusted Alone with a Pet?

Possibly. If the pet is very gentle and if you've seen no evidence of rough play in your child, then you can probably leave him unattended with a pet. However, if your preschooler has friends over, make sure the pet is out of the way unless you can be there to supervise constantly. Even if your own child plays gently with the family dog, a group of strange children can quickly get the animal overexcited. Even the most reliable old family pet may snap if pushed too far.

Can a Preschooler Be Trusted Alone with a Baby?

Not for long. As one parent put it, "My five-year-old could be trusted with a baby for about five minutes." A preschooler is likely to have better control over his violent impulses than a toddler, but he's still likely to be careless, a bit clumsy, and easily distracted. His curiosity about the baby may get the better of him if you leave them alone too long. Often a four- or five-year-old will try to be "helpful" by picking up or trying to play with the baby—with unintentionally harmful results. A preschooler who is put "in charge" of a baby outdoors in a fenced-in yard will quickly forget about his responsibility and let the baby go in the wading pool, eat sticks, etc. One mother cautions against leaving babies in infant chairs up on tables or counters when preschoolers are around. And, of course, your older children's small, breakable and battery-operated toys must be kept out of the baby's reach.

Can a Preschooler Ride His Tricycle Alone in the Street or Ride in the Street While You Supervise from the Sidewalk or Lawn?

No. The danger of cars even on the quietest dead-end streets is too great to take this kind of risk. A preschooler can quickly pedal away from you and into trouble, so it's important that you provide close and constant supervision for bicycle and tricycle riding. Give yourself a break by finding a quiet section of a park where your preschooler can ride around without traffic whizzing by. Many children will master a regular bicycle by the time they're five, but before their mastery is complete, there will be a long period of wobbling, falling, and crashing. Your supervision then is especially important.

Can a Preschooler Play Alone Outside?

Only if your yard is fenced in and you live in a safe, quiet neighborhood, and only if you are close by to check up frequently. Lewis, who lives in the Bronx in New York City, said his sons (ages eight and five) "definitely cannot" play outside alone, but Heidi, who lives in a small town in Minnesota, said she lets her five-year-old play in their fenced in yard unsupervised for short periods. "I'll go down to the basement to put in a load of laundry," she said. "I tend to do a lot of pacing back and forth to check up on her." Keep in mind that four-year-olds are notorious escape artists and commonly wander off to explore the neighborhood without so much as a glance behind. Marge, the mother of three, discovered her three-and-a-half-year-old son was missing one morning: he had escaped through the front door and walked a mile from home to "buy" some candy! (Nothing happened to him and the police brought him safely home.) So even if your child was a cautious homebody as a toddler, you may have to keep an extra sharp watch over him during the preschool years.

Can a Preschooler Tell the Difference Between a Poisonous and Nonpoisonous Plant or Berry?

Not reliably. Some children this age show remarkable talents for plant identification and will enjoy gardening or berry-picking with you. But even the most gifted, budding botanist has limited judgment and discernment. Thus you should always supervise a preschooler out in nature or in gardens containing poisonous plants.

Can a Preschooler Ride a School Bus Alone to Preschool?

Possibly—if the preschool has a private, reliable mini-van service. If not, it would be better, if at all possible, to hold off a few more years before allowing your child to ride a larger, public bus alone. Many pre-K kids ride public school buses to elementary school.

Childproofing Update

Childproofing for a preschooler tends to be more of an individual matter than childproofing for a toddler or infant. Statistically preschoolers are still in the highest risk group for household accidents; yet some preschoolers are much more reliable and responsible than others when it comes to household safety. If you are blessed with a cautious, obedient child, you can begin to relax *some* of your childproofing precautions.

One father said that when his son turned four-and-a-half they felt he was mature enough not to get into the kitchen cupboards, so they removed the locks. Debbie, the mother of two boys in a small town in Pennsylvania, said that her preschooler learned to pick the locks on the kitchen cupboards and open the safety gates just around the time she began to trust him on stairs and with potentially hazardous household products. As another mother put it, "My son [age five] can open the drawers with the safety latches, but he doesn't really take advantage of it. It's just not exciting to him." All three of these parents also pointed out that they make it a practice to discuss safety issues with their children on a regular basis; they can trust their children with *some* household hazards because their children are receptive to safety instruction.

However, parents of preschoolers who are not so easily guided need to be even more vigilant in their childproofing than they were during the toddler years. Staffs at poison control centers and hospital emergency rooms report that if a child has ingested a household poison once—and survives—he is very likely to do it again. It's up to you to deny him the opportunity by keeping your household hazards out of his reach: if he can pick the safety latches, move the hazards up to a high shelf; if he can get up to the high shelf on a chair or step stool, store them in a locked closet and keep the key with you.

Here are some of the childproofing precautions that all parents of preschoolers should continue to enforce:

Fire Safety:

Preschoolers must never be left alone when a fire is going in the fireplace, barbecue, or near a camp fire. It is especially important to keep matches well out of reach, since a preschooler is better able to strike a match than a younger child.

Stove Safety:

Similarly you should never leave your preschooler alone when the stove is on. Children this age love to "help" in the kitchen, and they actually *are* helpful in certain tasks such as mixing, measuring, cracking eggs. But allowing them to work around the stove when the burners are going or to open the door of a hot oven is simply too risky, even when you are right there.

Choking:

Preschoolers are long past the age when children routinely explore objects with their mouths—but that doesn't mean they are immune from choking on certain foods and household items. You should still be careful about leaving balloons (whether inflated or not) around preschoolers, and button batteries (the tiny kind you put in cameras, for example) are another common hazard. A safety rule in every household should be: No running or talking while eating. Be especially careful with hard candies, popcorn, nuts, and gum. For emergency treatment for choking, see In Case of Emergency, p. 0.

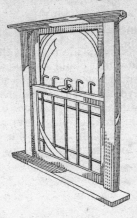

Cover windows with safety screens or gates.

Medicines:

Continue storing these in locked medicine chests or inaccessible shelves. A preschooler is *not* old enough to administer any medicine to himself. Continue to stress that medicine is not candy and avoid taking medicines, even aspirin, in front of your children.

Windows:

Since preschoolers are taller and heavier than toddlers, they are at greater risk of accidents involving windows. Regular window screens are *not* sturdy enough to resist the weight of a preschooler: to protect children from falls, cover low, accessible windows with safety screens or gates. Open double hung windows from the top only. Avoid sticking your head or arms outside a window (for example, to clean it) while your child is around.

Electrical Appliances:

A preschooler is much more adept than a toddler at "figuring out" how household appliances operate. But that doesn't mean she will use them safely. It's more important than ever to keep *all* household appliances, whether in the bathroom, the kitchen, or outside, away from preschool children. Unplug them when not in use, cover sockets so your child cannot plug them in herself, and if necessary, lock the appliances away.

Toy Update

Preschoolers adore their toys (and the toys of their friends and young cousins), and they have the manual dexterity and imagination to play for hours. A preschooler's increased coordination, memory, and concentration make it possible for him to play with a much wider range of toys than a toddler. Favorite toys of this age include puppets, dolls, blocks, cars, balls, and small plastic figures with which a child can act out imaginary scenes. If you have been assiduous in your safety discussions, your preschooler can be trusted to play safely with very small blocks, battery-operated toys (you should supervise at first and explain to your child that the batteries are *not* to be removed, and that the toys must not be put in water or left outside overnight), and more fragile toys than you would trust a toddler with.

However, there are still some important restrictions on the types of toys that a preschooler should have. Specifically never give a preschooler toys that contain:

• lead paint
• toxic or highly flammable materials
• sharp projectiles such as darts or missiles

- electrically operated parts, particularly heating elements
- sharp edges that could cut or points that could poke into ears or eyes
- glass or brittle plastic pieces that could easily splinter or break into jagged edges

The U.S. Consumer Products Safety Commission recommends these types of safe toys for preschool children:

- small wagons
- push toys such as child-size toy lawnmowers, shopping carts, vacuums
- doll carriages
- tricycles (for tricycle safety, see Chapter 5)
- bicycles with training wheels (starting at around age five)
- jungle gyms and swing sets (with adult supervision)
- solid wood and hollow cardboard blocks
- plastic press-together blocks
- puzzles
- pegboards
- magnetic boards with shapes
- sports equipment including balls, double-blade ice skates, sleds (without hand brakes or steering devices), soccer balls, softballs
- kites
- wading pools (with adult supervision)
- buckets, shovels, sand molds
- bubbles
- boat models (without sharp metal parts)
- realistic-looking dolls
- puppets
- dress-up costumes
- toy telephones
- arts-and-crafts materials including large crayons, magic markers, paints, easel, clay, chalk and chalkboards,

scissors with rounded ends, nontoxic paste and glue, beads, and string
- musical instruments, especially drums, tambourine, xylophone, harmonica, whistles, recorder, piano
- dominoes
- picture and color matching games
- learning games involving the alphabet
- simple computer programs involving color matching, learning letters and numbers (after age four)
- child's record player or cassette player (sturdy construction is a must; try to plug in electrically operated models in such a way that your child will not be able to unplug it easily)

If your preschooler insists on having toy guns or missiles, you must insist on getting him the kind that fire *soft* projectiles with no sharp edges such as ping-pong balls, soft-tipped darts, or helicopter-type projectiles. In warm weather or in bathtubs, water guns are a great way to permit safe fun with guns.

Activity Update

A preschooler is a child on the go. Parks. Pools. Play dates. Family vacations. Country and city outings. Birthday parties. Boat rides. Overnight stays with a favorite relative. All of these are activities that preschoolers enjoy—and all involve safety considerations that parents should be aware of. Even though you will *probably* find your preschooler easier to manage in new activities than he was as a toddler, you still have a long way to go before you can turn him loose with complete trust and ease of mind. Keep in mind that many accidents to preschoolers occur while you are right there with your child, but not paying full attention. Your presence makes the child feel safer, so he lets down his guard or is more daring than

Manufacturers' Labels: What Do They *Really* Mean?

Toy manufacturers are under no legal obligation to label toys with age recommendations, and when they do so, they are frequently motivated by marketing considerations rather than safety. A toy labeled "recommended for children three and older" may be safe for *some* three-year-olds but hazardous for yours due to small pieces, batteries, or other features that the label fails to mention. Try to assess whether these hazards are present before you buy the toy; if you have any doubts, don't buy it. Many parents assume that toys with no age labeling are appropriate for children of all ages, but this is not the case. Again, avoid buying toys—labeled or unlabeled—if you are unsure whether your child is old enough to play with them safely.

Some parents believe that their children are more advanced than the norm in every respect, and thus they feel they can disregard manufacturers' age recommendations when it comes to buying toys for their budding geniuses. Possibly, but certainly not reliably. The safest course is to assume that the manufacturer is right. If you're tempted to buy a toy that the manufacturer recommends for older children than your own, try to arrange for your child to play with the toy under your supervision—either in the store, or at a friend or relative's house—before you go ahead and buy it.

For more information about age-appropriate toys and to lodge a complaint about a toy that you feel has been mislabeled, contact:

U.S. Consumer Products Safety Commission
Washington, D.C. 20207
800–638-CPSC

he would have been on his own. Also, from age two on, boys are more accident-prone than girls.

Here are some of the other safety issues to consider as you accompany your preschool child on new adventures:

Use a snug-fitting jacket for any boat outing.

Water Safety:

The preschool years are a good time to start a child on swimming lessons, assuming she is willing. Look for a class in which the emphasis is on safety and water play; avoid classes that subject children to forced submersion or that have a high ratio of children to swim instructors. Remember, *even with swimming classes, a preschool child must never be allowed to play in or near water unsupervised*. A five-year-old who slips and bangs her head can drown in a wading pool just as quickly as a two-year-old. Remember also that young children tend to forget their swimming lessons unless they practice regularly. After a long winter away from the water, you may have to start from the beginning again. (For more about choosing and assessing swimming classes, see Chapter 5.)

Life Jackets versus "Water Wings"

If you plan to take your child on any kind of boat—be it a large fishing boat, a sailboat, or a canoe—it is essential that you buckle the child into an appropriate, snug-fitting life jacket. A life jacket is a buoyant vest that ties or buckles around the child's body and that will keep his head above water in case of a boating accident. Life jackets are *not* the same as the child floatation devices known variously as water wings, inner tubes, swim sweaters, or floaties. These are basically toys, designed to help your child stay above water while he plays in the pool—*but they are not substitutes for life jackets and they will not keep your child safe in the water.* In fact, many such devices will actually force a child's head *underwater* while it supports his arms and shoulders above water. Many public pools now ban water wings because they tend to give parents a false sense of security. This is a wise policy—and parents should *absolutely* ban such toys on boat trips. Life jackets, not water wings, are the safe way for a child (and an adult as well) to travel by boat.

Boat Safety:

Common sense should be your guide when considering a boating trip with a preschool child. How seaworthy is the vessel? How many adults will be on board to supervise the young children? How much sun exposure is your child likely to get? How dangerous are the waters? Shooting the rapids in a canoe can be a terrific thrill—but not with a four-year-old on board. If you are uncertain about the weather conditions or the safety of the boat or water, leave your preschooler home. When taking a preschool child on a boat trip, prepare him ahead of time by discussing boating safety, the hazards of horseplay on the water, the necessity for sitting quietly in a small craft, and the requirement of wearing a life jacket (see box above) at all times. Start with short trips and build up slowly if your child behaves well and enjoys these outings.

Play Dates:

As preschoolers begin to make friends, they will want to have play dates, either at your house or at the houses of their friends. This is fine, so long as parents are prepared to be extra vigilant when extra children are around. Our three-year-old, who never goes upstairs without permission, vanished there with her little pal within minutes of the other girl's arrival. Later, her friend insisted on going into the neighbor's yard while our daughter edged closer to the road, making it impossible to supervise them both, and the friend showed an aggressive interest in the newborn twins that made us a bit nervous. One good rule of thumb should be: never agree to a play date unless you feel willing (and able) to devote all your time to minding the gang. And before accepting an invitation for your child, ask the other parents a few questions about how they intend to keep track of the children. If you have any serious qualms about the situation at the friend's house, politely refuse the invitation.

Overnight Visits:

Most preschoolers are ready to go and spend the night with a favorite relative or to have that relative come and stay at your place while you escape for an adults-only vacation, business trip, or whatever. This is usually a wonderful experience for all concerned, but to insure that it's wonderful, you should keep a few safety matters in mind. Few relatives will take the time or trouble to childproof their houses for a short visit, but you might help them get rid of some of the major hazards. Grandma's handbag complete with pills, pins, and matches is a favorite target for young explorers, as are grandma's medicine chest, under-the-sink area, and grandpa's tool chest. Do whatever you can to childproof these areas or warn the relatives about the potential hazards.

Some children become wild when turned loose in someone else's house, and others are as timid as rabbits. If you suspect (or know) that yours are in the former category, take extra steps to discipline them before a visit and warn the relative of what havoc they are likely to wreak.

Whether the relatives are coming to your house or your child is going there, brief the relatives on safety rules and procedures just as you would a baby-sitter: just because they love the child doesn't mean they will remember all the routines necessary to keep him safe.

Parties and Holidays:

As children grow, they show a keener interest in going to parties and celebrating national and religious holidays, but you may have to be a little more careful about keeping them safe on these special occasions. For safety at Christmas time, see Chapter 3. The major hazard at July 4th celebrations are fireworks. According to figures compiled by the U.S. Consumers Product Safety Commission, an estimated 1,096 children under age five were injured in accidents involving fireworks during 1986. Many states outlaw fireworks altogether, but where states have not made laws, parents should. No preschool child should be allowed near fireworks, including sparklers, which can cause burns or ignite clothing.

Birthday parties can be lots of fun for preschoolers, but you should think twice about dropping your child off unsupervised at a large party or inviting loads of kids to your own child's party. If your child has a tendency to be wild and mischievous, accompany him to children's parties.

Parents who would never give their child a dangerous toy routinely purchase unsafe party favors because they're cheap and because they're regularly offered for sale. Watch out for party favors with small, swallowable parts, brittle materials, or jagged edges that could be poked into noses and ears. Never buy such favors for the parties you throw; and confiscate them as soon as your child receives them. Party favors are a particular hazard when younger siblings get their hands on them; so if you have toddlers or infants in the house, be especially vigilant about keeping unsafe party favors out.

Home Fire Safety

In 1988, 4100 Americans died in home fires, and 800 of these fatalities were children under age five (figures from the National Safety Council). Preventing home fires is up to *you*. Install smoke detectors in appropriate places around your home: at the top of flights of stairs, in the kitchen, near the furnace, near bedrooms. If you have any doubts about the wiring in your home or in your home appliances, have it checked out thoroughly by a licensed electrician. Keep fire extinguishers handy in the kitchen. Check them periodically to make sure they are working. Never leave matches or lighter fluids in places where children can get at them and be especially careful with cigarettes.

Although fire prevention is your responsibility, your children—including preschoolers—should be carefully instructed about what to do in case of fire. The basic message you want to impart is: if there is a fire in the house, you should escape. Stage family fire drills at intervals in which you run through the procedure to evacuate the house in case of fire. Explain to your child the location of preferred fire exits. And pose "What if . . . " questions to see how well your child is catching on: What if you heard the alarm go off and you tried to open your door and it felt hot? What if the hall was on fire but the stairs to the basement were not? You might have to explain to a child that certain safety rules—e.g., never go outside without permission, never open or lean out your bedroom window—may be broken in the event of fire. Obviously a three-year-old is going to have a hard time opening his ground-floor window and jumping out in the event of a fire in the hall outside his bedroom, but a sturdy five-year-old just might succeed at this if he has been carefully instructed.

Keep in mind these tips for preventing and escaping from home fires and go over them with your children:

- If a room is filled with smoke, crawl along the floor.
- If your clothes are burning, cross your arms over your chest (to keep flames from reaching the face), drop onto the floor, and roll around and around so as to smother the flames. Practice the rolling technique together. It also helps to roll up in a rug. *Never run when clothes are burning.*
- If a room is smoky and it's hard to breathe, open a window for air. Smoke, not the actual flames of a fire, is the cause of the majority of deaths in home fires.
- Do not extinguish kitchen grease fires with water: instead use salt or baking soda for small kitchen fires or a proper fire extinguisher (look for the label of the Underwriters Laboratories—UL—or Factory Mutual—FM).
- In case of an electrical fire, first cut off all electricity in your house by pulling the main switch. Extinguish flames with a dry-chemical fire extinguisher, *not water*. Avoid electrical fires by never overloading circuits, replacing fuses promptly, and repairing frayed electrical cords at once.

Discussing Safety

Talking about safety is more important than ever with a preschooler, and it's more rewarding too because information, rules, and directions are really starting to sink in now. Preschoolers seem to ask *why?* with every second breath, and you can use this natural curiosity as a way of introducing safety topics and explaining the reason why certain things are unsafe, off-limits, etc. You may soon find your preschooler walking around parroting your instructions, "Jumping in the tub is dangerous . . . ," "Baby sister must not have my Tinker Toys because she'll choke . . . ," etc. And your lessons may work so well that your preschooler may begin to correct *your* unsafe behavior. My preschool-age daughter seems extremely alarmed whenever I go near the barbecue and warns me repeatedly about how I'll get burned unless I'm careful.

Basically you should use the same approach in discussing safety with a preschooler that you used with a toddler: introduce safety topics in a low-key way, don't lecture or sit the children down for an "important discussion," keep discussions brief and focused on one issue at a time, use songs and games whenever possible to get the message across and help them remember it. I found that discussions of personal privacy worried my three-year-old daughter until I began to sing a silly song when I dried her after her bath: "Your body is your own, your body is your own, And you can always say to anyone, 'Just leave me alone!'" I felt a little dumb about it, but she seemed to enjoy it and respond much more favorably than she did to my other attempts to engage her on the topic. Other parents have used similar approaches to discussing street crossing, car safety, bike and fire safety. Let the circumstance and the activity dictate when and how to bring up safety issues. Don't make the mistake one mother made of sitting her daughter down the day before kindergarten and going through a lengthy checklist of safety topics that she had never mentioned before. Work these discussions into your everyday life with your child.

Safety issues you should bring up with your preschool children include:

- personal privacy
- how to act around strangers
- sexual abuse
- tricycle and bicycle safety
- safe behavior away from home—at friends' and relatives' houses, for example, and at birthday parties
- safe behavior in preschool

- safety in public places including parks, public transportation, city streets, shopping areas
- safety with younger siblings
- safety around pets—both your own and the pets of strangers
- water safety, at pools, beaches, and in boats
- safety outdoors, whether in the yard, in the woods, or on camping trips
- travel safety—in the car, in motels, in restaurants

For more information on discussing safety with children, see Chapter 6, and see Chapter 8 for how to discuss the dangers of sexual abuse. Even more than with toddlers, "What if . . . " word games and books are excellent ways of introducing safety matters to preschool children.

As our children grow up, many of us oscillate between anticipation and nostalgia. Anticipation of the time when they will be more self-sufficient, easier to care for, less in need of our attention and vigilance. Nostalgia for the old days when we could still pick them up and cuddle them, when they were sweet little babies who never shouted *no!* and never demanded junk food and new toys, when keeping them safe was as simple as popping them in a crib or playpen. The preschool years may be the time when such parental oscillation is most intense. All traces of the babe in arms have vanished from our preschooler—and yet in so many ways this whirlwind of energy, daring, whims, and demands needs *more* attention, more monitoring, more forethought, and more imagination on our parts to keep safe. Just wait! As parents of older children never tire of telling their comrades one rung down on the parental ladder: For every safety matter that disappears, three new ones crop up. Once children are out in the world of school, they face an entirely new set of challenges—and we face a new set of challenges to keep them safe. Meeting these challenges and helping our young school-age children learn safe habits and make safe choices is the subject of the final section of this book.

Part Four

Out In the World: The Early School Years, Ages Five to Seven

10. Trust, Responsibility, Independence

The beginning of school is a great watershed in the lives of children and their parents. And it is a watershed as well in the realm of safety. As your child steps out into the wider world, her freedom increases and your direct responsibility for her safety wanes. Gradually, but inevitably, she is going to shoulder the responsibility for keeping herself safe—by deciding to obey the safety rules you have made and discussed with her, by making sure the choices she has learned are the safe ones, by understanding when she can handle a situation on her own and when the wiser course would be to appeal to you, to her teacher, or to some other responsible adult for help. Obviously this is not going to happen when she is five; even when she is seven and ready for second grade, the transition will still be in its early stages. "It can be a difficult time," said a New Hampshire mother of a six-year-old daughter, a toddler, and infant sons, "because they are getting so much more freedom, but you still have to protect them." You *do* still have to protect them, but you also have to begin to let go of them, and this can be even more difficult for some of us. But it's necessary and, in the long run, it's the safest course. Acquiring the skills, the knowledge, and the judgment to keep oneself safe is one of the basic necessities of growing up. Imparting these skills is one of our major goals as parents.

Encouraging our early school-age children to assume this responsibility can be a lot trickier than buying an infant a safe crib or explaining to a toddler why he shouldn't touch the stove. Complex issues of trust, mutual respect, setting and testing limits, and openness in communicating arise. It's important for parents to gauge their child's readiness for new activities and for a child to feel that he *can* inform his parents when he has gotten into trouble, when his friends are pressuring him to do something unsafe, when he has failed through carelessness, inattention, or just bad luck. An early school-age child needs and seeks out challenges—and it's up to the parents to determine which challenges are appropriate, to provide the right level of supervision, to know when to say yes, and how to say no. More than ever, our five-to-seven-year-olds need us to set safe examples for them.

The balance of responsibility between a maturing (but still young child) and a beleaguered (and frequently worried) parent can be delicate, and progress may occur in fits and starts. Maintaining that safe balance, charting a child's progress, knowing the common safety pitfalls of the age and how to avoid them, is what this chapter is all about.

Trusting Each Other

Trust and responsibility work two ways. If you trust your child, she is more likely to live up to your trust. If you give her more responsibility, she is likely to act more responsibly. The problem is knowing where to draw the line between freedom and safety. To some extent we can take our cues from our children and from their peers. If your seven-year-old is begging to ride her bike around your quiet residential block and if other children her age are doing this, it might be a good opportunity to trust her. On the other hand, common sense will tell you when a child's demands are unrealistic or downright dangerous. A first-grader who has taken karate lessons after school is *not* as invulnerable as he thinks and claims he is. Just because all the other children routinely play in the road doesn't make it safe or acceptable for your child. No child should be trusted in a situation that is inherently unsafe.

In deciding how much freedom to give, be attentive to your child's behavior, how she makes decisions, how she follows your direction. One mother said her son who was overly outgoing with strangers as a preschooler is now very cautious, in part because of safety instruction at school. She feels she can give him more freedom now in public places such as stores or the post office. Helen said her seven-year-old has always been very gentle and protective with his younger sisters (ages four-and-a-half and two), and she now feels she can leave her son alone in the house with them, for fifteen minutes to a half hour, while she is out in the yard doing chores. However, she strongly feels that children should not be called on too often as baby-sitters for their younger siblings, and that in any case, seven is much too young to be a reliable child minder. Pamela agrees; she trusts her six-year-old son not to hurt his baby sister (age nineteen months), but she says he tends to forget about her and go off with his friends when they're playing in the yard together. Karen's kids can't wander out of her yard because it's fenced, but the six-year-old twins sometimes forget to come get her when the eighteen-month-old twins (yes: she was doubly blessed twice!) go near the wading pool, so she has to keep an eye on them all.

It also makes good sense to prepare your child for any new responsibility by discussing the situation carefully ahead of time. "What if . . . " questions can be a good way of determining how your child would handle herself and how much she understands about potential hazards she might face.

A few of the common situations in which parents generally begin to trust their early school-age children include:

- Bath: Soon after age five, most children can look after themselves safely in the bathtub or shower. (Whether they'll do a decent job washing themselves is another matter altogether!) Start off by leaving your child alone for short periods while you remain within earshot. If all goes well, gradually increase the time. A good rule of thumb is that if a child can run his own bath competently, he can be allowed to bathe in privacy.

- Unattended play in yard: This really depends on your neighborhood, your yard, the street you live on, the children who are likely to be out. Five-year-olds are *generally* less likely to wander off than four-year-olds, so if you live on a quiet block in a safe area, you can begin to trust your child outside by himself starting with short periods of time. Karen, who lives outside Mobile, Alabama, said she lets her older children play alone in their fenced-in yard, but she has a rule that if anyone comes up to the fence, including another child, they must go inside and get her. Families who live in cities, high-crime neighborhoods, or on major through-streets must wait a good deal longer before letting children play alone outside the house.

- Crossing streets: Again, it depends on the street and the neighborhood, as well as such factors as the weather and the time of day. Six or seven-year-olds can probably cross quiet residential streets in daylight to go to friends' houses, but you might want to watch them the first few times to make sure they stop and look both ways for cars. An occasional reminder of pedestrian safety is essential (see Chapter 5 for more on safety for child pedestrians). The greatest number of child pedestrians are killed when they run into the road without looking and when they dart out from behind a parked car or between parked cars—so these situations should be the focus of your concern. Statistically the child pedestrian most likely to be hit by a car is a boy, age 7.3, who is crossing the street (but not at an intersection) between 2:00 and 7:00 P.M.

When you're at the stage of deciding whether or not to trust your child to cross the street, go out walking with him and let him be the one to decide when it is safe to cross and where. If he makes safe choices consistently, he's ready. Twilight, dawn, and, of course, nighttime are *not* safe times for children to be crossing streets alone.

Helen, who lives on a very quiet street in a small town in Maryland, says her seven-year-old lacks the "car sense" she acquired at a young age growing up in urban Baltimore. Though she trusts him in their neighborhood, she feels she has be extra cautious when she takes him downtown because he is so sheltered from traffic.

You can't teach a child about pedestrian safety from inside a car, with a book, or with a lecture. You can only teach him by doing it together, hundreds and hundreds of times in many different situations.

• Riding bikes: By around age five or six, having wheels of one's own becomes a tremendous status symbol for kids and one of their primary sources of entertainment. By around age seven, if your child is now very steady on his bike and if your neighborhood streets are safe and free of heavy, fast-moving traffic, you might consider letting him ride around on his own. (If you live in a city or near a major traffic artery, try to find a park, playground, or empty parking lot where your child can ride around away from traffic.) Again, start off with small distances—maybe to the corner and back—to see how he does. One Florida mother of a six-year-old said

Put reflecting tape on the fenders of your child's bike.

she lets her son ride "only as far as he can hear my voice when I call him." A cautious New Hampshire mother lets her six-year-old daughter go only as far as the next house.

Also keep in mind these bike-safety tips:

—Buy a bike that is the correct size for your child now, not one she will grow into. Attaching blocks to the pedals is *not* a safe way of adjusting the bike to the child.

—Dirt bikes with thick wheels are steadier than ten-speed bikes with skinny wheels. A well-made second-hand bike is going to be sturdier and safer than a flimsy new one.

—Make the bike easy for cars to see by attaching a bright-colored flag to the rear of the bike and putting reflecting tape on the fenders.

—Light-colored clothing makes the child more visible to motorists. Long pants and sleeves offer some protection to accident-prone kids on two-wheelers.

—Some dogs are bike chasers. Teach your child *not* to panic, but to maintain his normal speed and ride calmly away without screaming at the dog or attempting to kick it away.

- Helping in the kitchen: Some parents let six- and seven-year-olds use the stove, but they always supervise to some extent. One mother lets her six-year-old son cook eggs but she turns on the stove, puts the butter in the pan, takes the pan off for him, and turns off the stove. In another household, the six-year-old may not use the stove but is allowed to use the microwave. Another mother lets her child cut things, but only with a butter knife. A good rule for stove safety is that children should *not* be permitted to cook on the burners if they are too short to reach them. Placing a child on a stool next to the stove is really asking for trouble. If your first-grader wants to bake, let him mix the batter, pour it in the pan, and then call you when it's time to put the pan in the oven. Food processors and blenders should probably be off-limits for some years.

- Using electrical appliances and tools: You can probably begin to let your child handle some electrical appliances and tools, but supervision is still necessary. Marge plugs in the hair dryer for her six-year-old, turns it on, and lets her daughter use it; when she's done, she calls her mother to turn it off and unplug it. Child-care author Penelope Leach recommends letting young children handle power tools like electric drills (*turned off*) to see how heavy they are and letting them see how they operate (with you holding the tool well away) so they understand how fast and sharp they are. When children become strong enough to use some power tools themselves, you *must* be there to supervise because, as Leach puts it, "young arms tire and attention wanders, but by doing it *with you* she will learn the safe way to do it without you later on" (*The Child Care Encyclopedia*, Alfred A. Knopf, 1984). Obviously heavy equipment like lawn mowers or chain saws should be off-limits for some time to come.

• Staying home alone: Some seven-year-olds *may* be ready to stay home alone for short stretches of time during the day, but leaving a seven-year-old alone at night while you go out to dinner or whatever is definitely *not* a good idea.

Discuss the idea with your child ahead of time if you think she's ready (girls do mature physically and emotionally faster than boys, and so are likely to be ready sooner). Think about how well she follows your safety instructions, how she handles herself with friends, how responsibly she acts with her siblings. Before you leave her on her own, show her where emergency numbers are posted, review fire exists and escape routes, and make sure she understands certain ground rules, including no cooking, water play, or trips outside the house. Also discuss telephone procedures for handling emergencies. Ask her, "What would you say if someone called while I was gone?" Correct answer: "My parents are busy and can't come to the phone right now but I can take a message." Wrong answer: "My parents aren't here now, call back later." (One seven-year-old girl, who answered the call I placed to interview her mother about safety, said, "My mom's *really* busy now so she can't come to the phone." Her manner and tone of voice were so convincing and self-assured that I had a complete image of her mother whipping up a souffle with one hand, feeding the baby with the other, and learning French from an audiocassette. When I called back the next day, I was really surprised when the mother told me she was actually out shopping and her daughter was home alone. It might make sense to rehearse your child in adopting a similar assured, unhesitating tone.) If the strange caller persists or tries to draw her into a long conversation, she can just hang up. Also ask: "What would you do if someone knocked on the door?" Correct answer: "I would not open it." She can talk through the closed door to anyone who has come with a delivery, and instruct the person to leave it outside. If the person won't go away, your child should call the police.

When you come back, ask how she felt about being on her own. If she says she was frightened and upset (or *seems* that way), you should not repeat the experience for some time. (For more about children at home alone, see the section on latchkey children in Chapter 11.)

By all means do not push your child into this situation prematurely. If she's not ready or willing, hold off.

No Unsupervised Swimming or Boating

Your five-to-seven-year-old is definitely *not* ready to be trusted to swim alone or with peers. No matter how well he swims and no matter how long he has been swimming, he needs *your* supervision when he is in the water. That doesn't mean you must be in the water with him every moment, but you should be around the pool, lake, or ocean to keep an eye on him—and the larger and rougher the body of water, the closer you should be in attendance. Many parents have a rule that children may not go in the water without first asking permission, and they must ask *each time* they want to go in. Pools and beaches are obviously safer if there are lifeguards on duty, but that doesn't mean you can go entirely off duty yourself. Your child's safety in the water is *your* responsibility and should remain so until he reaches nearly adult size, strength, and endurance.

Supervision is also essential for all boating activities, and life jackets are as important as ever. No matter what your seven-year-old says or how bitterly he complains, he *needs* to wear a life jacket if he is in any type of boat. And, for that matter, you do, too. (For more about life jackets and boating safety, see Chapter 9.)

Friends

By the time a child reaches school-age, her friends begin to play a significant role in her life. In terms of safety, friends can be a boon or a threat, depending on their behavior, their upbringing, their habits, and their interaction with your child.

Your school-age child, by and large, *chooses* her own friends (or they choose her). For better or for worse, you are going to have less and less control over her choices. But you still do have *some* control, and you should try to exercise it carefully. As one mother of a seven-year-old pointed out, "My parents always put in their two-cents worth about my friends and they were always right, but I'm really hoping not to do that. I don't make too many comments. I'm afraid that if I express dislike, it might push my son closer to the child I disapprove of. I try to limit myself to comments on the unsafe *actions* of his friends."

Tactful discussions can work wonders with early school-age children and are usually more effective than ultimatums or threats. If you feel your child is being pressured by his friends into behaving unsafely, talk it over with him. It might also help if you discussed the situation with the parents of his friends. If you really feel the friends are bad for your child, say "no" to play dates and explain your reasons.

Remember that not all peer pressure is bad, as Vicki Lansky points out in her useful book *Practical Parenting Tips For the School-Age Years* (Bantam Books, 1985). Kids need to fit in and as long as they are fitting in safely, you should let them. But when other kids are pressuring your child to participate in unsafe activities, he should know that he doesn't always have to follow the herd or follow the leader. Try to save your battles for the most serious situations—for example, swimming unsupervised, playing with fire or fireworks, riding bikes in forbidden territory. Your goal, of course, is to make your child not only behave safely himself but to influence his friends in safe behavior. As one mother put it, "I feel that my son is more a positive influence on some of his wilder friends than they are a negative influence on him." This kind of confidence comes from years of building trust, talking over safety, setting safe examples—and from just having a good kid.

Sometimes a bully or trouble maker will attach himself to your child and your child will passively put up with it. You can help by explaining that it's okay to drop a friend he doesn't like; and if possible, you might go out of your way for a few days to help him avoid this unpleasant child. Tell your child to use you as an excuse ("My parents won't let me . . . ") to get out of activities that either he doesn't want to participate in or you feel are unsafe. Saving face can be incredibly important in a child's world.

Remember that children this age still need *some* supervision and limits in their play. All too often we let our older children disappear with their friends into back bedrooms, basements, yards, while we deal with younger children, chores, or carry on our own social lives. Children can egg each other on in unpredictable ways, and mischief that your child would never have contemplated may be promptly instigated by her friends. One mother said her six-year-old daughter is friends with an aspiring nurse who tried to take blood from her with a sewing needle. Another told a story about a neighbor's usually reliable seven-year-old who took a notion to open the attic windows while her toddler siblings were playing up there. A Florida mother said her seven-year-old is exposed to older children who are much more daring than he and who occasionally play with matches. Extra parental vigilance might have prevented *some* of these situations. Punishment, discussion, and clearly delineated rules will probably keep most of them from recurring.

They Can Hear—But Are They Listening?

Many parents of early school-age children report that discussing safety (and everything else) with their children is actually *more* difficult than it was a few years back. The problem is not lack of comprehension or lack of experience, but lack of attention. Children this age are notoriously distractable—and even when they're not distracted, they act as if they are. Or they make believe they're listening—"Oh sure, Mom, right, whatever you say"—when they're actually thinking about something else. "We talk about safety, but I wonder whether I'm really getting through" was a comment several parents made. It may take a little more imagination on your part, a little more perseverance, and a lot of repetition to get the message across. Keep safety discussions brief and to the point. "What if . . ." word games and even pop quizzes might be useful in finding out how much your children are taking in. Offer rewards for correct answers. Television shows feature all sorts of hazardous situations and, since our children do pay attention to their favorite programs, you might use them as a way of focusing your child's attention on safety issues, at least for a few minutes.

Providing Safe Challenges

There's a special glow of pride that suffuses the face of a child who has successfully accomplished a new and challenging task or activity. His expression fairly radiates: "Wow! Look at me! I really *am* big enough now!" Children grow and learn through challenges—and it's one of the essential ways they find out about safety. As one parent put it, "I believe nurturing independence is one of the most important things. If you are overprotective, they don't learn to deal with their own problems." By sheltering our children from new experiences, we are also sheltering them from the opportunity to extend their judgment, their self-awareness, and ultimately their ability to care for themselves. We may not feel entirely comfortable about giving our permission the first time, but in the end we have to admit that it's worth it.

This is not to suggest that we accede to their requests to go on wilderness hikes without adults, to jump on subways, to attend the movies downtown with their friends, or to throw unchaperoned slumber parties. Nor does it mean that we should push our early school-age children to tackle more challenging situations than they are ready for. The seven-year-old boy who hid under the covers during the hour he was left by himself at home would clearly have been better off with a baby-sitter. The six-and-half-year-old girl who wept through the youth-group camping trip would have had a lot more fun if her parents had waited three or four years. Again, common sense, a good assessment of our children's abilities, and careful attention to their requests (and their fears) should be our guide.

Here are some of the safe challenges that parents of five-to-seven-year-olds said their children carried out successfully and happily:

- Kay lets her seven- and five-year-olds (boy and girl) run into the post office by themselves to buy stamps, affix them properly to envelopes, and put the letters in the proper slots. (The children have been well instructed about strangers, and she is waiting in the car nearby.) She also lets them go into small stores, such as the pharmacy, to pick up things. She still worries that they won't find their way around big stores such as supermarkets.

- Marge lets her six-year-old daughter go to the concession stand with a friend at the small lakeside beach near her home in New Hampshire. Since the lake is visited mostly by families and people who know each other, she also lets her daughter use the public bathroom there by herself: "I tell her to go right in and come right back." From years of low-key discussions, her daughter is aware of the dangers of strangers and sexual abuse.

- Donna lets her daughter, just six, walk a few aisles away from her in the supermarket, but she prefers to keep an eye on her, and the girl also prefers to be fairly near her mother in public places. Because they live on a nature sanctuary in Massachusetts, Donna feels her daughter knows more about identifying plants and berries than many children her age. She thinks her daughter will soon be ready to go berry picking without adult supervision.

- Karen feels that her older children (ages eight and six) could travel on planes by themselves, although the opportunity has not yet come up. (For more on children traveling alone, see Chapter 11.) She also gives her six-year-old twins a fair amount of responsibility in caring for the eighteen-month-old twins, for example, feeding them bottles and changing their diapers.

- Karen also gave some good examples of challenges that she feels her children are *not* ready for yet. Her six-year-old son has asked to "camp out" unsupervised in a tent at his friend's house because his cousins have done it, but she said no. Her children have also asked to be allowed to go off by themselves at the mall and then meet up with her at a prearranged time, but again she feels they're too young. Her daughter, who has just turned eight, wanted to go to the movies with a friend, but Karen offered to rent them a video instead and let them watch it all by themselves. "Maybe I'm wrong to be so protective," she says, "but that's how I feel."

Setting Safe Examples

"Setting safe examples is *extremely* important," said a mother of a six-year-old. "They learn by examples at this age.'' ''They watch everything I do,'' said another mother about her five children, and thus the example she sets has a major impact on their behavior. Several parents brought up instances in which their early school-age children actually *corrected* them when they slipped up in safety. ''The other night someone knocked on the door at ten in the evening,'' recounted the mother of five, ''and I let him in without saying 'Who's there?' They reminded me how bad this was. They also let me know when I left scissors out on a counter for the baby to get at.''

Parents have singled out these areas as especially important in setting safe examples for their early school-age children:

- In the car: always buckling their own seat belts, driving within speed limits, not cursing or screaming at other drivers.
- Around water: wearing life preservers in boats or canoes, obeying pool rules, not having heavy meals right before swimming.
- With tobacco and alcohol: not using these when the children are around or using them with moderation and safety awareness. Many children learn of the dangers of substance abuse in school. ''My daughter thinks smoking is tacky and that beer is a drug,'' said one mother. ''She is very aware of our habits in this regard.''
- With drugs: avoiding all illegal and dangerous substances.
- With fire: always lighting and extinguishing fires safely, using tongs and pot holders around the barbecue, using matches safely and correctly. One book suggests *teaching* kids the safe way to light matches (striking away from the body with the matchbook or box closed) so if they do ever light them, for example, on a camping trip, they'll know how.
- In the kitchen: handling knives and appliances safely, using pot holders when cooking at the stove, using and storing cleansers safely.

- With strangers: treating strangers the way we want our children to treat them, with courtesy but caution. Most of us talk to strangers more than we think our children should; but if our children observe this, we can explain the ways in which we were careful. We can also explain to our children that we are less vulnerable to strangers than they are. One father said that both he and his wife talk to strangers as part of their jobs—he is in adult education and she is in retail sales. "It's hard to tell our daughter not to do that when it's what we do for a living. Instead, we tell her to be careful." Her parents also remind her that she must be even more careful about strangers when she is by herself or with peers.

It often helps children this age take notice of our safe examples if we point out our behavior in specific instances and explain the reasons for it. Donna said she tends to keep up a running commentary in the kitchen of why she uses pot holders, why she turns pot handles back, how to light the stove, etc. When she holds the ladder for her husband in the yard, she tells her daughter why this is so important. We may feel a bit foolish repeating the same safety instructions time and again, and our children may get a bit sick of hearing them—but it's one way to insure that the message *really* sinks in. If we can get our five-to-seven-year-olds to imitate our safe examples, there's a good chance that younger children will imitate the safe examples set by older brothers and sisters. So we may be setting up a chain of safety from which the entire family will benefit.

11. Safety in a Wider World

An early school-age child is like an explorer just sighting the New World on the horizon. So many new activities are opening up for him, so many new skills are being acquired, so many dreams are being fulfilled and new dreams and schemes being hatched. Chances are that his "journey" to school is his first taste of real independence—a daily excursion in which he is entirely on his own. And after school, there are friends' houses to visit, sports to play, and during vacations there are trips to take, cities to visit, trails to hike, lakes to plunge into. By age seven, he may be taking his first unaccompanied plane ride. And, if both of his parents work, he may be shouldering the considerable responsibility of the so-called latchkey child.

The changes come at a dizzying pace at this time in a child's life, and at times they may be too much to handle. Our young adventurers still need our guidance and our protection, sometimes more than ever. We need to walk them through the safe procedures for getting to school; we need to take a long, hard look at our neighborhoods to assess just how safe they are for child pedestrians and bike riders. More than ever, we need to warn our five-to-seven-year-olds about strangers. When we take our kids to the beach, to the woods, or simply into someone else's yard, we need to prepare ourselves and them for possible hazards such as strong tides, mosquitoes, poisonous plants. Latchkey children and their parents need to know a set of basic rules, and so do young unaccompanied travelers. There is no question that safety remains a major issue and a major challenge now, as it was in infancy, toddlerhood, and the preschool years. Our reward for rising to the challenge is seeing our healthy, happy, and safety-conscious children enjoy their new world to the fullest.

Getting to School

School safety begins with *getting to* school safely. Of course, the safest way is for you to drive your child to and from school yourself, but this may not be feasible; it's certain to be inconvenient at times, and it may deprive your child of valuable experience in looking after herself and in socializing with other children. For each of the other means of transportation—walking, school bus, riding a bike, carpooling—there are a number of special considerations to keep in mind to make the experience as safe as possible.

One consideration that applies to all methods of transport is to make sure both your child and the school know where and how he is supposed to go at the end of the day. Children must be instructed *never* to go off with anyone after school, even a close relative or friend, and never to take a detour to the candy store without your permission and prior knowledge. If there is to be any variation in the routine—for example, the child's aunt will be picking him up instead of the school bus—notify the school ahead of time to avoid mix-ups. Many schools have a policy that the parents must give their permission in writing that same day for any change in normal transportation procedure. If your child's school does not have such a policy, you may want to try to implement one.

Walking:

In order to walk safely to school, your child must know how to cross a street alone, how to use sidewalks or, if there are no sidewalks, how to walk on the side of the road, how to deal with strangers, and how to act in case of emergency. Some children will be ready for this earlier than others; and, of course, a great deal depends on where you live. Even in a quiet small town or suburb, if there are no sidewalks along the route to school the risks of a pedestrian accident are significantly increased. Karen said the subdivision outside Mobile she lives in has no sidewalks but lots of teenagers drag racing, so she really has to lecture her three school-age children about street safety. Don't pressure your child into walking to school alone: wait until she says she's ready and asks to do it.

Also consider these safety pointers:

- Determine carefully what the safest route to school is. Choose a route that is the most direct and the least secluded; has the fewest number of potentially dangerous intersections, e.g. intersections with many turning cars or converging lanes of traffic; has sidewalks running along it; has the most traffic police, school patrol officials, or crossing guards; has the greatest number of other children using it; has the fewest number of obstructed views.
- Even before school starts, accompany your child on this approved route several times until you're certain she understands it perfectly. Point out landmarks, street crossings, etc. It might help at first to draw a large map of the route and let her carry it with her. Karen walked

her six-year-old twins to their school for two weeks and then watched them without them knowing it to see how they did.

- In some communities there is a block parent program in which adults who are at home during the times children go back and forth to school agree to be available to children in distress. They display a symbol in their windows so that children know which houses to go to in case of trouble from a stranger, a medical emergency, or merely when they're frightened. Point out these houses and the symbol they display to your child. If such a program does not exist in your community, point out houses of neighbors or storekeepers whom you know you can rely on.

- Introduce her to the school-crossing guards, regular traffic police, and any other public safety personnel she is likely to encounter along the route.

- Well before the school year begins, make sure you have reviewed street crossing (including use of sidewalks, crosswalks, and how to cross with the light) and safety with strangers (particularly never to approach a car when a stranger calls to her). Don't wait until the day before school for a huge lecture on all the perils she might face. (For more about strangers, see below.)

- Make sure your child knows her home address and phone number, knows how to make a phone call from a public phone (rotary dial *and* push-button), and knows where to reach you—or another trusted, reliable adult— during the times she is walking to and from school.

- Your child will be better off walking to school with a "buddy," assuming that her buddy is a cautious, responsible child.

- The American Automobile Association runs a "Safest Route to School Project" to assist parents and teachers in instructing children in safe habits in walking to and from school. Get in touch with a local chapter of AAA, or have your child's school do so, to find out more about this project. The AAA also publishes a series of books

Teach your child to cross in front of the bus so the driver can see her.

for children about pedestrian safety. Useful titles for children walking to school are *How I Cross a Street*, *Traffic Signal Lights*, and *I Listen and Look for Cars Coming* (AAA 1976).

School Bus:

School-bus safety means getting to and from the bus stop safely, knowing how to get on and off the bus, and knowing how to behave on the bus. Walk your child to the bus stop a few times before school starts so he becomes familiar with the route. If the stop is a long way away, draw a map and point out houses along the route with the block-parent symbol in the window (see above). It is sometimes possible to get the school bus to stop closer to your home if you apply a little gentle (and persistent) persuasion (when I was a child, my family "bribed" the driver with homemade pies so he would pick up and deliver us door-to-door). You obviously want your child to be on time for the bus, but try not to get her to the stop so early that she's the only one there for a long stretch of time.

If possible, try to wait with your child the first few

times to instruct her how to get on and off the bus safely. Tell her to stand well back as the bus pulls into the stop, to enter the bus single file, and to keep her hands, arms, and feet away from the closing door. When she gets off the bus, she should step right up onto the sidewalk or curb (in any case, *out of the street*); if she has to cross, she should cross in front of the bus so that the driver can see her. Remind her to look both ways before crossing.

You obviously have no direct control over how your child behaves once he gets on the bus, but you do have some influence. If the children are rioting on the bus, it's obviously going to make the driver's job a lot tougher— so instruct your child to sit at all times, not to shout or throw things, and certainly not to race up and down the aisle. It is particularly important that the children remain seated until the bus comes to a complete stop, so they won't get thrown forward. Tell your child to keep the bus aisle clear of books, lunch boxes, etc. and not to stick her arms or head out the bus window.

Some schools give each child a printed set of rules for bus behavior, and you might want to review these rules with her carefully. If she is being tormented by rowdies on the bus, she can complain to the driver or the proper school authority. Sometimes the "bad" kids congregate in one section of the bus (often the back), and your child can stay out of trouble by avoiding that section. If there are not enough seats and she must stand, she should always hold on to a strap, handle, or the back of a seat.

What if she misses the bus? For safety sake, you're probably going to have to go to some trouble and expense to get her to school—by taxi, by driving her yourself, by arranging for some friend or neighbor to drive her. For the sake of future behavior, you should make sure she pays the consequences—taxi fare out of her allowance, extra chores in return for driving time, or privileges revoked.

If she gets on the wrong bus on her way back from

school or if she somehow misses her stop, the safest course is usually to stay on the bus and return to school, where she can call you from inside the school or perhaps get on a later shift of the correct bus. Tell her to inform a teacher or school guard of what has happened.

Car Pool:

The same car safety rules that apply to your own car should apply to a car-pool situation: most essential, all children must be buckled up at all times. Once children weigh over eighty pounds, they can use adult seat belts (a shoulder harness is safer than a lap belt), but until then they should, if possible, be buckled into an appropriate car booster seat or booster (see Chapter 9 for a discussion of car seats). If necessary, show the other car-pool drivers how to buckle your child into his seat; and always make sure you use the seats correctly for other children. If using your child's car seat proves to be unfeasible in the car pool, at least make sure that he rides with a seat belt at all times.

Car-pool drivers need to take special care when discharging and picking up riders, especially in bad weather. Try to choose a pickup and drop-off spot on the same side of the street as the school, but well away from the school-bus loading zone. Never discharge passengers into the middle of the street or signal them to race across the street while you are double-parked or blocking traffic.

You will drive better if the children are behaving themselves, so try to think of some ways to keep them quiet and under control. Word games or sing-alongs may occupy them for the duration of the ride. Firm commands may be necessary now and then, but for a real troublemaker the best course may be to talk to the child's parents.

Make sure you always obey school-zone speed limits.

Bike:

Unless your child's school is quite close and can be reached on quiet streets with light, slow-moving traffic, a bicycle is *not* recommended as a way for him to get to school. Not until he becomes a teenager does a child have sufficient judgment and strength to handle his bike in traffic, and even then, as anyone knows who has tried to pass a cyclist on a busy artery, a bike rider is exposed to considerable danger. For more about bicycle safety, see Chapter 10.

Learning "Street Smarts" About Strangers

Many parents of early school-age children put strangers at the top of their list of safety concerns. It's easy to see why. A child starting school is much more exposed to the outside world than a child at home; and a five- or six-year-old is still a young and vulnerable child. Even though the statistics tell us that our children are much more at risk from car and pedestrian accidents than from the advances of strangers, it is still natural for us to be especially sensitive to this issue when our children start school. Just as children can learn to be safe pedestrians, they can learn to take some control in keeping themselves safe from strangers.

Children exercise their control over strangers by saying *no*. It's as simple as that. "Don't talk to strangers" is the first rule that occurs to most of us when we contemplate the subject; but an even better first rule is: "Don't go with strangers." As Penelope Leach points out in *The Child Care Encyclopedia*, "The child who is forbidden to speak to anyone he does not know is actually at a disadvantage in learning to keep himself safe in his community.... If he is reluctant to speak, he cannot ask the way when he is lost or even respond civilly when asked the time.'' The safe child is one who keeps a wary distance between himself and a beckoning stranger; who refuses to approach a car when a stranger calls; who knows that the only correct response is *no* when a stranger makes a tempting offer. The safe child also knows which strangers to appeal to in case he needs help: a uniformed police officer or school guard; a uniformed store security guard or clerk (the people who work at the cash registers and wear name tags), or, if no one else is available, a parent of small children.

One situation early school-age children are commonly confronted with is an offer of a ride from someone who claims to be (and may actually be) a friend of the family. Your children should know that the answer to such an offer is *no* (or "No thank you, I'd rather walk" in the case of adults they recognize) and that they should come right home and tell you about it. Also teach your children to stand well back and out of reach if anyone stops in a car and tries to talk to them.

Help your child avoid contact with strangers by showing her areas she should stay away from: empty lots, parking lots, alleys, entryways and stairways of apartment buildings, schoolyards after school is over, wooded areas. Children are safer in groups, so try to arrange for your child to have a "buddy" with whom to walk to and from school, or even better an older child or sibling.

In keeping your children safe from strangers, you should also bear in mind these tips:

• Strangers use all sorts of ploys to attract the attention and win the confidence of children. They might ask for help, claim they have been sent by the child's parents in an emergency, or even claim to be a police detective investigating a case of shoplifting. Talk over these situations with your child so she will be prepared. Tell her that trustworthy adults do not ask children for help. In all cases, her gut feeling should be: "I don't know you and I'm going to stay away from you no matter what you say."

- Children tend to trust and obey people who know their names. Warn your child that a stranger might try to find out her name by calling out to her, "Hi Jenny!" and then waiting for her to correct him. You should take care not to display your child's name on the outside of her lunch box or clothes.

- Remind your child that she can always say *no* and walk away from anyone. Drum this in through repetition and practice if necessary. This may be a particularly difficult lesson for a shy child or one brought up to be obedient to adults.

- Have your children practice shouting, "That is not my parent!" and explain to them that this is the best thing to shout if someone tries to grab them. People might assume that a child shouting, "No, get away from me!" or "Leave me alone!" is merely having an argument with his parents.

- Teach your children to fight, squirm, kick, and scream if someone tries to grab them. Have you ever tried to hold onto a six-year-old who is fighting with all his might to squirm out of your grip? It's not that easy. A first-grader who has studied martial arts is not going to be a match for a 180-pound child abductor—but his self-defense skills may buy him the few seconds he needs to run away. And that's the point of a child fighting back: to gain the time to run for help.

- If a stranger does manage to lure your child into his car, tell your child to stay calm and make sure not to buckle the seat belt. As soon as the car pulls off the road and stops, your child should try his best to run away and shout for help.

- Keep close track of your children's whereabouts and make it a family rule that they are always to ask permission before going off somewhere. Parents in safe, sheltered neighborhoods, tend to be a bit lax in this regard. As one mother from a quiet suburb put it, "I always knew my seven-year-old was at one of three houses, but I wasn't always sure which one." Instead of wondering and worrying about it, she has made a rule that he must let her know where he is at all times.

- If your child does encounter a stranger who gives him the creeps—for example, someone hanging around outside the school or someone he has noticed cruising slowly around the neighborhood—the best bet is *not to attempt to hide*, but to get away fast and tell a responsible, trusted adult about it. The overwhelming majority of street crime occurs by chance: a victim happens to fall into the path of a mugger, child molester, etc. Teach your children to stay out of the paths of such people; and when they spot a suspicious character, to put as much distance between them and the stranger as possible.

- Teach your children how to make telephone calls for help, where to call, and what to say. Practice, if possible, on pay phones, both a rotary model and a pushbutton. In some areas a call to the local-police precinct will bring help faster than a call to 911; if your child is in doubt, he can always call 0 for the operator. Rehearse with your children how to report a dangerous situation: they should give their names, tell the police clearly and precisely what has happened, and describe where they are (they can look for street signs and landmarks).

- Ask your local librarian for recommended books for early school-age children on the subject of strangers. A few widely available books include: *Stranger Danger* by Patricia Ryon Quiri and Suzanne I. Powell (Julian Messner, 1985), *The Street Smart Book* by William Marsano (Julian Messner, 1985), *Safety Zone* by Linda D. Meyer (The Chas. Franklin Press, 1984), and *Play It Safe* by Kathy S. Kyte (Alfred A. Knopf, 1983). If your child reacts badly to a particular book, look for another one or discuss the subject in a gentler, less alarming manner.

For more about keeping children safe from strangers and from child sexual abuse, see Chapters 6 and 8.

Child Abduction: Prevention and Taking Action

The term "child abduction" conjures up an image of a deranged criminal jumping out at a child from a darkened alleyway. But in fact, the person most likely to abduct a child is not a stranger but the divorced parent who has lost custody of the child. According to a report entitled "Missing, Abducted, Runaway, and Thrownaway Children in America" issued by the U.S. Department of Justice in May 1990, in 1988 there were 354,100 "broad scope" family abductions (both serious and minor incidents) compared to 3,200 to 4,600 non-family abductions. Of this latter figure only 200 to 300 were defined as "stereotypical kidnappings," i.e., long-term, long distance, or fatal episodes. These are the first "hard" national figures we have in this area, and they clear up previous misconceptions that family abductions ran as high as 750,000 per year and non-family abductions as high as 7,000.

Julie Cartwright, director of media relations for the National Center for Missing and Exploited Children in Washington, D.C., notes that the most encouraging findings in the Justice Department study are that there were 114,600 failed *attempted* abductions (most involving an attempt to lure a child into a car). All of these involved strangers. Cartwright, however, points out that " 'Stranger' is not really an accurate term for non-family abductions because the children are probably familiar with or befriended by the abductor in some way before being kidnapped. We try to get parents to be wary or alert to strange *situations* as opposed to strange-looking people. The kidnappers are not people hiding under bridges or wearing trench coats." The child abductor, like the child molester, is likely to "stalk" the child and befriend him without the knowledge of the parents. The abductor has thus ceased to be a stranger in the child's mind, and the child is more vulnerable. The skills children need to protect themselves against abduction are similar to those they use to avoid sexual abuse—never keeping secrets from their parents, having the confidence not to be threatened or bribed into silence by an adult, feeling they can discuss *anything* that is bothering them with their parents (see Chapter 8 for more about preventing child sexual abuse).

Protecting a child from abduction by a noncustodial parent is in many ways more difficult. It is important to notify the school—including the child's teacher and the school principal—promptly about a divorce and to make sure the teacher sees a copy of the custody decree (such abductions usually occur right after the divorce and custody settlement, so do not delay). If you suspect that your ex-spouse may try to abduct the child, you might show a photo of your ex-spouse to teachers, school-crossing guards, etc. If you are concerned about abduction, do not send your child to school on foot or on the school bus: drive her if possible or arrange for a trusted friend to drive her and pick her up. Make sure the school knows that she can only be released to you or to a person you designate. Discuss the situation with your child and, if you have real cause to be worried about abduction, warn her about what her noncustodial parent might try to do. Reassure the child often that you love her and want her to live with you; warn her that her noncustodial parent might tell her that you no longer want her around but this is *not* true.

In order to minimize the risk of noncustodial parental abduction, as well as to safeguard your child's relationship with both parents, try to stay on good terms with your ex-spouse. The booklet *Parental Kidnapping: How to Prevent an Abduction and What to Do If Your Child Is Abducted* put out by the National Center for Missing and Exploited Children suggests that custodial parents try to keep the issues of child support and visitation separate. It is not uncommon for a custodial parent to deny visitation rights if support payments come late or do not come at all—and the noncustodial parent may then retaliate by snatching the child. For more information on parental kidnapping, contact:

The National Center for Missing and Exploited Children
2101 Wilson Blvd., Suite 550
Arlington, Va. 22201

If your child is missing, notify your local police force quickly. They will ask you for a full description of the child, a current photo, and any other identifying information. Make sure they supply this information to the FBI's National Crime Information Center computer, a central data bank of information on missing children that federal, state, and local law enforcement agencies around the country can tap into. If for any reason the local police fail to enter your child into this computer, you may contact the FBI yourself at 202–324–3000. Put up fliers around your neighborhood, city, or community with your child's photograph, a description, and the number of the police department that an individual should contact in case he or she has seen the child (to avoid crank callers, do not give your home phone). Before hiring a private investigator, check out the individual's credentials *carefully* with the state licensing agency, the Better Business Bureau or the Consumer Protection Office for information.

There are two organizations that have hotlines to assist parents in finding missing children:

The National Center for Missing and Exploited Children
800–843–5678

Child Find of America
800–426–5678

Parents might also want to contact:

Adam Walsh Children's Fund
11911 U.S. Highway 1, Suite 301
North Palm Beach, FL 33408
407–833–9080

The Missing Children Help Center
410 Ware Boulevard, Suite 400
Tampa, FL 33619
800–872–5437
813–623–5437

National Crime Prevention Council
The Woodward Building
1700 K St.
Washington, D.C. 20006
202–466–6272

Safety Outdoors

We tend to think of the great outdoors as a place of magic, release, inspiration, and just plain fun—and it certainly can be all of those things. But the outdoors, whether a wilderness area in a national park, a patch of woodland at the edge of town, or a local park, does have certain potential hazards that we need to protect our children from. This becomes much more of an issue during the early school-age years when our children tend to spend more time outdoors with less direct supervision.

Camping and Hiking Trips:

If you are taking young children on a camping or back-packing trip, even for a very short time, you must take certain precautions. Make sure you have extra warm clothes (wool keeps you warm even when it's wet), extra food supplies, rain gear, warm sleeping bags, a flashlight, whistles (one for each child in case someone gets separated), matches, a good working compass and map, and a first-aid kit. Leave word of your exact intended route at a ranger station or park authority. Find out whether the water in streams is safe to drink before drinking it or letting your child drink it.

You must discuss the vital importance of *staying together on the trail* with young children. Often our five-to-seven-year-olds are far swifter hikers than we are, especially if we're lugging a sixty-pound backpack; or reluctant young hikers may lag far behind. Unless they are properly warned, children may become separated from the group and get lost. It happens all the time—and not just to children, but to experienced campers. In the wilderness, there is safety in numbers, and children must be made to understand this. If you are hiking with a large group, set up a buddy system.

If your child does get separated from the group, tell him to stay put until someone finds him. He can signal to the others with a whistle, flashlight, or reflecting mirror. Explain to children that they can relax the rules about never talking to strangers if they need help finding you. A stranger can be their means of rescue.

Bad weather:

Severe weather conditions can also pose serious dangers on hiking and camping trips or simply when children play or walk outdoors. High mountainous areas may be quite cold even in the middle of the summer, and the combination of cold, rain, and exposure may bring on hypothermia, rapid heat loss from the body that could be fatal. If your child complains of feeling chilled, shivers uncontrollably, or becomes sluggish, it is essential that you act quickly to restore his body warmth. Shelter him from wind and wet, get him into dry clothing, wrap up his head, and keep him warm. Do not rub the child's body to try to restore warmth and do not give him anything to drink. One good way of restoring body warmth is to let your own body act as a radiator through skin-to-skin contact. Even better is to place the child between two warm bodies. You should arrange for medical attention as quickly as possible.

In extremely cold weather, you must be careful about frostbite. To prevent frostbite, keep children's extremities well-covered with woolen socks, mittens, and hats and insist that your children come inside when they are tired and chilled. Frostbite and chilling occur more rapidly when there is wind. If any part of your child's body becomes frostbitten, it will turn red at first and then become white and numb. Keep the frostbitten part warmly covered until you can get the child indoors, and then gradually warm it by immersing it for short periods in lukewarm (not hot) water. Once sensation returns, the child should move and wriggle the part to restore circulation. Treat the frozen tissue with extreme gentleness. Do *not* rub it with your hands or with snow since this may cause serious damage to the tissue.

You should also know and tell your children how to get shelter in a thunderstorm: if the car is nearby, get in it and stay there until lightening stops; the woods are safer than open fields since lightning strikes the highest object; however, if you have taken shelter in the woods, do not touch wet trees since the water on their bark can conduct electricity; do not take shelter under an isolated tree or near a fence made of metal; get away from water, whether a pool, lake, stream, or ocean and do not seek shelter in places where water might collect; if you are caught in an open field during a thunderstorm, *crouch down* on the ground with your hands on your knees, so as to minimize the "target" you are presenting to lightning.

Farm and woodland animals:

City and suburban kids will need special instruction about behaving around animals before a hiking or camping trip, or a trip to an agricultural area. The animals that they may encounter in the wild, or even in barnyards or roadside fields, are *not* like the animals in petting zoos. In most cases, a wild animal will only let a human approach if it is sick, and even if it can't get away, it can probably still bite. Snakes should *not* be handled, nor should your child attempt to feed or pat farm animals. (Remember also that many fields are enclosed with electrified fences that could give your child a painful shock if he touches it.) In certain areas of the West, bears have become a menace to tourists: if you keep your distance from bears and take care not to leave food near where you sleep, bears will leave you and your children alone.

Biting and stinging animals:

If the skin is broken by a bite from any animal, whether it's wild, domesticated, or a family pet, the child should be taken to the doctor. You can take immediate action yourself by washing the wound carefully with cold water and covering it with a sterile bandage. Calm the child down and have a doctor check the wound.

Insect bites are unavoidable in many parts of the country, but most bites merely cause discomfort, swelling, and itching. Bring along some calamine lotion or cortisone cream (to be used sparingly on children) to ease the pain of bug bites. If your child is stung by a bee, try to pull the stinger out with a tweezer, but do not squeeze or rub the raised area around the sting since this will release more of the venom. Apply ice or cold water to the sting if possible.

Ticks pose a greater danger than mosquitoes and bees because they may carry two very serious illnesses: Rocky

Mountain spotted fever and Lyme disease. If you are in an area infested by ticks, you must check yourself and your child at least once a day: check every part of the body, especially legs, the groin area, armpits, and the scalp. The deer ticks that carry Lyme disease are not much bigger than a grain of sand, so they may be extremely hard to spot. If you find a tick, the safest procedure is to pull it off slowly with a tweezer (make sure you get the head); then either burn the tick or flush it down the toilet. If a tick bite develops into a spreading skin rash or a child develops flulike symptoms several days after the bite, go at once to a doctor for treatment.

More serious bites such as snakebites or jellyfish bites require prompt medical attention. Not all snakebites contain venom, but since you can't be sure, the safest course is to get the victim to a hospital emergency room at once. Make sure the child does not move the limb that has been bitten since this will spread the venom: carry the child to your car or to an ambulance. If your child is stung by a jellyfish, remove as many of the tentacles as you can with a towel or stick (do not use your bare hands). Pour alcohol over the area where the sting has occurred. A child who

---

Kite Safety

An early school-age child is old enough to fly a kite by herself as long as she follows a few basic rules:

- Kites should never be flown in areas where there are power lines, telephone lines, or antennae.
- If a kite becomes tangled in a power line, it should be left there. The child should *not* try to tug it down or climb up to free it.
- Safe kites contain no wire or metal, either in the kite itself or in the string used to fly it.
- Kites must be perfectly dry when they are flown.
- Flying a kite in a lightning storm is dangerous, and Ben Franklin was lucky he didn't get electrocuted.

is in serious pain or who develops a skin rash should be taken immediately to a hospital. If the reaction is mild, you can treat the child yourself by spreading a paste made of baking soda and water over the area, leaving it for an hour, and then scraping it off.

For more about treating these and other emergencies, see In Case of Emergency on p. 00.

For a list of poisonous plants, see Chapter 3.

Water safety:

If you and your family spend any time around water, your children should learn how to swim. Knowing how to swim will not "drown proof" children as some classes claim, but it will certainly increase their margin of safety. However, no matter how well they swim, early school-age children will still need your personal supervision whenever they go in the water. Relying on a lifeguard is not good enough.

A child who is accustomed to swimming in pools will be in for a big surprise when she first swims at an ocean beach, a river, or even a large lake. The force of ocean waves or river currents can easily overpower even the strongest adult swimmer. You must take particular care on any tidal body of water: rising tides can cut off your access to safe shoreline in a matter of minutes. River currents may be gentle close to shore and brutally swift just a few feet out. Lakes tend to have currents of much colder water flowing through the deeper sections. There may be rocks or tree stumps concealed a few feet below the surface of a river or lake. It can be extremely difficult to judge the depth of any natural body of water. Explain these potential hazards carefully to your child and supervise her closely whenever she is around a lake, river, or the ocean.

One necessary article for safety on boats is a properly fitting life jacket. A child should be instructed to remain

If a child falls through the ice, he should stretch his arms over the solid ice and kick his legs behind him as if swimming.

seated at all times on a small boat, and he should know that if the small boat capsizes or tips, he should remain with the boat.

Sports Safety:

In the hot summer months, take care that young children engaged in active sports do not get heat exhaustion, a condition marked by dizziness and possible fainting from loss of body fluids. A child playing a very active sport such as basketball or soccer should take frequent breaks in the shade. Keep children well hydrated by insisting that they drink plenty of liquids. A child is safer with sports equipment that fits properly than with oversized hand-me-downs. Protect children from sunburn by covering exposed skin with sunblock or suntan lotion with a protection factor of fifteen or higher. Reapply the sunblock after the children have been swimming or if they have been sweating a lot. You'll have to be more assiduous about protecting a fair-skinned child from the sun, but a dark-skinned child may need protection too.

If you live in an area in which the children ice-skate on frozen ponds and lakes in the winter, you must be very careful that the ice has frozen to a sufficient depth to support skaters. In some areas the local police will post warning signs when the ice is still too thin. In the absence of such a service, you should test the ice yourself before letting children skate. From a safe position near shore drill a hole through the ice and measure its depth. Ice must be four inches thick to support skaters. In the event that a child does fall through the ice, the correct way for him to get out is to get his arms up onto the still intact ice, spread his legs out behind, and kick with them as he would in swimming. In this way, the child may be able to haul himself up onto the solid ice; and if the ice keeps breaking before him, he will at least be moving toward shore.

Travel Safety

Most airlines now allow children as young as five to travel unaccompanied, but before packing your child off, you must carefully consider whether she is mature and confident enough to handle such a venture. As a general rule, five is much too young for solo air travel—seven is probably the safe minimum age. Before the trip, spend some time preparing your child by "talking her through" each step of the journey, from boarding, to meeting the flight attendant, to fastening her seat belt, to the noise and possible ear discomfort she may experience on take-off, to the use of an air-sickness bag, to eating her meal off a tray, to deplaning and meeting up with the party at her destination.

Always be certain to alert the airlines in advance that your child will be traveling alone. When you take her to the airport, make sure that the plane will leave on time; if it has been delayed, wait with her and notify the party that is going to meet her at the other end. When you check your child in for the flight, you will have to fill out a travel card giving your name, address, and phone number and that of the party who will be meeting up with her on the other end. Accompany the child to the gate, where the gate attendant will help her board, and remain at the airport until the plane takes off. Then return home so that you can receive a call from the airlines in case of a mishap.

On the plane itself, a flight attendant will look after her, helping her find her seat and probably checking up on her frequently to make sure she is doing okay. General airline policy is for a flight attendant to deliver the child to a gate agent, and for the gate agent to request correct identification and signature from the person designated on the travel card before releasing the child. Sometimes airlines are lax about enforcing this policy, so you might want to insist on it when you help the child board. Even though she will have the protection of the airplane's staff, it couldn't hurt to review stranger safety with her beforehand. If at all possible, arrange to have your child fly on a nonstop or direct flight; making a connection involves too many unknowns and possible complications, and on many airlines a child must be eight or older before she will be allowed to fly on a connecting flight.

For more information on helping children fly safely, write for a copy of a pamphlet called "Kids and Teens in Flight" put out by the Department of Transportation. Send a stamped, self-addressed envelope to:

Department of Transportation, Room 10405
400 Seventh Street Southwest
Washington, D.C. 20590

Unaccompanied travel on buses and trains is not recommended for early school-age children, and in fact, Amtrak has set eight as the minimum age for a child traveling alone, and then only during daylight hours and with the approval of the station master. Children as young as five are permitted to travel alone on Greyhound and Trailways buses, but only on trips shorter than five hours that do not involve a transfer. In addition, the parent must arrange for the child to be met at her destination. In the event that you feel your child is ready for a bus trip alone, make sure you board the bus with the child, introduce her to the driver, and help get her settled before the trip begins. Seat the child as close to the driver as possible so he can keep an eye on her. Tell the driver where she is supposed to get off and ask him to make sure she in fact gets off the bus at the correct stop.

School-age children are usually great fun on family vacations—they really enjoy going to new places, having new experiences, exploring new horizons, sometimes even sampling new foods. Keeping them safe in strange places does, however, involve a little extra vigilance on our part. Remember if you are taking your youngsters abroad, that they will not be able to read street signs, understand what people are telling them, or make themselves understood. This, of course, does not apply in Great Britain, but there you have the problem of traffic moving in the opposite direction to what we are accustomed to. Children (and adults, too) will need repeated warnings to look the *other* way before crossing.

Children from the country, small towns or suburbs may need a few lessons in street safety and street smarts before a trip to a large city. Marge, who lives in a small town in New Hampshire, reported that her otherwise cautious six-year-old daughter panicked in New York City traffic during a family vacation. Her reaction to seeing taxis speeding down the avenues was "Let's run!" Children must be warned not to flash wallets or money around and to be careful of pickpockets on crowded city buses.

For safety on hiking and camping vacations, see above.

At some resorts and on some cruise ships, there are special "camps" or groups for children. These can be terrific or pretty awful depending on the staff, the facilities, the activities, and how well your child adapts to new experiences. Do set aside some time at the start of your vacation to check out the situation, interview the staff, observe the group in action, and to discuss your child's reaction to the program. Close, conscientious supervision is especially important if the children will be playing near water. If your child cannot swim, you would be unwise to let him join a large group at a pool or ocean beach. For children ages five to seven, the ratio of counselors to tots should be about one to seven or eight. Make sure someone on the staff is trained in CPR (cardiopulmonary resuscitation) if there is to be swimming or even beach activities.

Latchkey Children

According to some estimates, as many as one-third of all American elementary-school students are latchkey children, that is, they come home from school to an empty house and spend a considerable amount of time each week at home alone. In most cases, the reason for this arrangement is that both parents work outside the home. Few would deny that children ages five to seven are too young to look after themselves reliably and safely (to say nothing of the emotional problems and loneliness that latchkey children face), but in many families there is no alternative, or at least the parents have not been able to find an alternative.

Finding such an alternative should be a high priority of parents of five- to seven-year-old children in self-care. Are there day-care centers where your child might go after school for a few hours until one of you gets off work? Does the school run any programs before or after regular school hours that your child might be enrolled in? Would your company consider offering after-school care? Have you explored a flextime arrangement with your employer so that one of you can be home when the children return from school? Is there a neighbor, perhaps someone who is retired, who might come over and mind the children for a few hours every afternoon? or a reliable high-school student? It may take quite a bit of legwork on your part to make alternative arrangements, but it's worth pursuing, at least until your child is older and more mature.

If, for whatever reason, you are going to continue with the latchkey arrangement, keep these rules in mind and review them frequently with your child:

- Your child must come directly home after school (or get your permission that day for any change in plans). When he gets home, he must be sure to lock the door behind him.
- If anything looks suspicious at home—for example, the front door is ajar or a strange car is parked in the driveway—your child should *not* check it out himself, but should get to a neighbor's house or pay phone and call you for instructions.
- Your child must know how to take phone calls without revealing that he is home alone. The standard line is, "My mother is busy right now and can't come to the phone. May I take a message?"
- Similarly the child should not open the door to any callers, but should speak through the door and instruct them to come back later, leave the package outside, or whatever.
- Stay in close touch with your child over the phone. Have him call you as soon as he gets home and whenever something comes up. Some children also appreciate it when their parents leave little loving or humorous messages around the house.
- Make sure there is a complete list of necessary phone numbers (your workplace, police, doctor, fire department, trusted neighbor, etc.) next to the phone. Have your child practice making emergency calls in front of you to see how he does. If necessary, rehearse the procedure often to keep it fresh in his mind.

- Children who openly display their keys are asking for trouble. If keys are worn around the neck, they should be hidden under clothing. If possible, arrange for neighbors to have a spare set of keys or hide a key outside in a place where no one would think to look and where no one can observe your child getting it.

- Make sure your child has change for making phone calls from a pay phone (and knows how to do this) in case he is locked out.

- Latchkey children tend to get into trouble when they are bored, so it's a good idea to structure their time with a mix of fun activities and chores. Plan a few surprises for your child, such as special snacks or new games. Reward good behavior and chores well-done with praise, treats, or whatever reward is meaningful to your child.

- Prepare food ahead of time that requires no cooking, or minimal cooking. If your child will be doing any cooking at the stove, make sure he knows how to use a kitchen fire extinguisher.

- Don't just *tell* children what to do in case of a fire or other home emergency; *practice* the correct procedures with them. Stage make-believe fires, break-ins, etc. and run through the situation until they get their "part" right.

- If there is more than one child at home, you're going to have to set down firm rules about fighting. Encourage children to write down their disagreements for your attention later, rather than fighting about them when they are home alone. Older children will naturally have to spend some time looking after younger ones, and they should be rewarded for doing this, with gifts, praise, stars on a star chart, extra allowance, extra television, special privileges, or whatever is meaningful to them.

- Your child should know how and where to call for help in case of a medical emergency. All too often, injured children wait for their parents to come home when they might save valuable time themselves by calling an ambulance.

- Some schools and organizations such as the Boy Scouts or the Camp Fire Council offer programs and publications for latchkey kids in self-reliance, home safety, caring for younger siblings, and other common issues. Both you and your child might profit from such a course or booklet.
- In some areas there are hotlines for children at home alone who need help, support, reassurance, or just someone to talk to.

For more about the issues of latchkey children along with some practical tips on keeping them safe, see *The Handbook for Latchkey Children and Their Parents* by Lynette and Thomas Long (Arbor House, 1983).

Afterword: Onward and Upward

Safety, as you have gathered from reading and using this book, enters into almost every aspect of being a parent. To begin with, safety is a matter of details, hundreds and hundreds of details about everything from setting up a crib to hiking up a mountain, from baby proofing a kitchen to showing a child how to walk to school. Nearly every activity our infants, toddlers, preschoolers, and early school-age children engage in brings up some safety concern, and for every concern there is information for us to apply and rules for us to learn and to teach our children.

The details are important, there is no getting around it, and mastering them may be particularly difficult when we first become parents and everything is so new to us. Who had any idea that a nine-month-old would learn to climb steps overnight? that a toddler could outsprint his mother in a parking lot? that a preschooler's promise to stay put cannot be relied upon? that a six-year-old would assume that by "stranger" we meant someone who looked like Darth Vader? As they grow, our children teach us nearly as much as we teach them. In time, between what we learn from them, what we pick up along the way, and what we find out in books like this one, the details of safety become second nature. We grow a second pair of eyes in the back of our heads. We learn to anticipate. We remember the proper equipment, the suitable outings, the limits of endurance, both theirs and ours. Safety becomes instinctive. The process of learning new details and applying new safety information never really stops—it just becomes built-in.

Part of that process, a part that becomes ever larger and more important as our children grow up, is building safety awareness into *them*. Teaching our children about safety is not, as this book makes clear, a one-shot deal. It is not a matter of delivering a long lecture, making lists, threatening them with dire consequences. It is something we do all the time, a little at a time, whenever the opportunity presents itself, by setting good examples, by practicing with them, by drawing the safe moral from some situation in real life or on television, by reading and singing and standing on our heads if necessary. Children who have been taught well and taught carefully about safety are not scared of the world around them; they take risks, after due consideration; they welcome challenges, but they know their own limitations and the limitations of the people and circumstances around them. And perhaps most important of all, when they're not sure, when they're confused, or when they need to know more, they come to their parents to talk things over. As our children grow, teaching them and reassuring them that they can come to us—even when they have done or have witnessed something wrong—becomes central to their safety. And then, at some point in adolescence, they pass beyond doing what we let them do and begin to do what they want to do.

Ultimately, whether we like it or not, their safety is going to be in their own hands. They are going to be "out there" in the world facing many complicated and potentially dangerous situations and temptations at a much younger age than we faced them, if we faced them at all. Drugs and alcohol, sexually transmitted diseases, street crime, driving or being driven by friends. These are some of the safety challenges our children will face in the future. And, most likely, they will face these challenges alone. At seventeen, at twenty-seven, they might still come to us for advice, for consolation, for money just as they do at seven—but when it comes to safety, their choices and actions are really in their own hands.

That's why it's vital now, when we have so much influence and so many opportunities, to make safety not only *our* second nature but *their* second nature as well. The awareness of safety and the safe habits we help our children develop in their early years will stand by them all their lives. Safety is one of the many gifts we parents have the privilege of bestowing on our children.

In Case of Emergency

Emergency Numbers
To Be Posted by the Telephone:

Pediatrician:
Alternate Physician:
Police:
Local Precinct:
Local Ambulance Service:
Hospital Emergency Room:
Fire Department:
Poison Control Center:
Neighbors to help in case of emergency:
Your work number:
Your home phone number, address, and cross street:

Cardiopulmonary Resuscitation—CPR

CPR is a way of breathing for a child and stimulating
his heart to continue beating in the event of certain emer-

gency situations, including near drowning or suffocation, choking, smoke inhalation, and severe infections blocking the respiratory tract.

To be certified in CPR, you must receive nine to fifteen hours of training through courses offered by the American Heart Association or the American Red Cross. Some hospitals and adult education programs also offer instruction in CPR.

You cannot master the CPR techniques merely by reading about them. You can only master them through course instruction and practice. If you have young children, you or your spouse or both should enroll in a course in CPR. The illustrations and guidelines that follow are intended as a *review* and a *reference*—not as a substitute for a CPR course.

Before starting CPR for a baby or child who is choking on a foreign object, it is essential to dislodge the object. You cannot breathe for a child unless his air passage is clear.

How to Help a Choking Infant (up to one year of age)

1. If the infant is coughing or gagging, do not interfere. He may cough the object up without your assistance.
2. If the infant cannot cough up the object and stops making any sound, have someone *call for an ambulance*.
3. While waiting for the ambulance, try to dislodge the object yourself:

    —*Position the baby on your arm:* Place the infant face down on your arm with one hand supporting the jaw and chest. Support your arm on your thigh. Make sure the baby's head is lower than the chest.

    —*Deliver back blows:* Using the heel of your free hand, hit the baby firmly and rapidly four times between the shoulder blades.

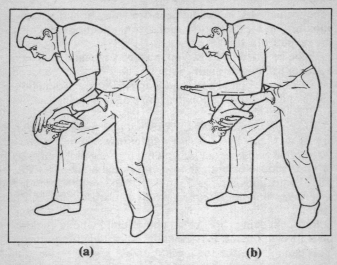

(a) (b)

(a) Place baby down on your arm with one hand supporting his jaw and chest. Make sure the baby's head is lower than the chest.
(b) Deliver back blows using heel of your free hand.

—*Turn the infant and deliver chest thrusts:* Carefully turn the baby and support him faceup on your arm with his head lower than his chest. To locate the correct spot for chest thrusts, draw an imaginary line between the nipples and place your fingers one finger's width below this spot. Using the tips of two or three fingers, compress this spot four times. Press downward with your hand coming in from the side, *not* running vertically up the baby's body.

Press with force but not so hard you hurt the baby.

—*Repeat:* If the object does not come out, turn the baby and deliver four back blows with your hand again. Turn back and deliver more chest thrusts. Repeat until the object is dislodged.

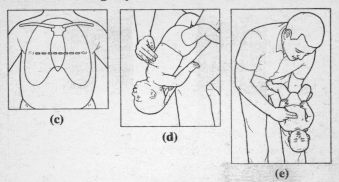

(c) Locate position for chest thrusts. Imagine a line between the nipples.
(d) Place the tips of two or three fingers below this spot.
(e) Give four chest thrusts with hand coming in from side.

—*Remove the object:* Remove the object by sweeping it out of the baby's mouth with your finger. Do not poke your finger deeply into the baby's mouth. Only attempt to sweep out the object if you can *see* it.

Breathing For an Infant

1. Before starting artificial respiration, try to rouse the baby by shaking and pinching him or flicking the soles of his feet. If he does not respond in ten seconds, have someone *call for an ambulance immediately.*
2. Position the baby on his back on a hard surface.
3. With one hand on the baby's forehead, gently tilt his head back. This will open the airway. Keep your hand on his forehead to maintain this slightly tilted back position.
4. Look to see if the baby's chest is moving; listen for sounds of breath; feel for air on your cheek. If there is

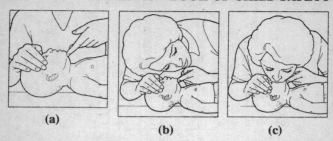

(a)

(b) **(c)**

(a) With one hand on baby's forehead, gently tilt his head back to open airway.
(b) Check for breathlessness for three to five seconds.
(c) Cover baby's nose and mouth with your mouth and give him two slow puffs of air.

no sign of breathing in 3 to five seconds, begin breathing for the baby.
5. Cover the baby's nose and mouth with your mouth to make a tight seal and give him two gentle breaths of air (about the amount of air you can hold inside your cheeks). Remove your mouth to get each breath, but make sure you do it quickly. Keep the head slightly tilted back by holding your hand on his forehead. If the baby's chest does not rise and fall with the gentle breaths [reposition head], his air passage may be blocked and you need to clear it as described above in "How to Help a Choking Infant."
6. Check for a pulse at the inside of the baby's upper arm using your fingertips. Take your time: an infant's pulse is difficult to feel.
7. If there is a pulse but the baby still is not breathing, continue giving him artificial respiration at the rate of one gentle breath of air every three seconds. Keep breathing for the baby until help arrives or until he can breathe by himself.
8. If there is no pulse, begin stimulating circulation with chest compressions (see below).

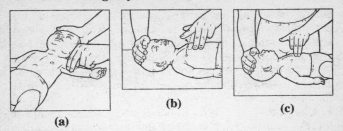

(b)

(c)

(a)

(a) Check for pulse at the inside of baby's upper arm.
(b) Locate the correct spot for compressions. Draw an imaginary line between the baby's nipples. Place the tips of two fingers one finger's width below this line.
(c) Give five compressions followed by one gentle puff of air.

Stimulating Circulation For an Infant Whose Heart Has Stopped

1. Begin with artificial respiration as described above. You should already have called for an ambulance. After breathing, check for the baby's pulse carefully at the inside of his upper arm. Take up to ten seconds to feel the pulse—an infant's pulse is easy to miss.
2. If there is no pulse, position the baby on his back on a firm level surface with one of your hands holding his head in place to keep the airway open. His head must be level with his heart.
3. To find the correct spot for compressions, draw an imaginary line between the baby's nipples and then place the tips of the index and middle fingers one finger's width below this imaginary line.
4. With your fingertips on the correct spot, compress the baby's sternum a half-inch to an inch five times in succession and then give the baby one gentle breath of air as described above in "Breathing For an Infant." You

should be giving the baby a total of *ten* cycles of *five* compressions to *one* breath or a total of *fifty* compressions and *ten* breaths per 30 seconds. Work quickly as you alternate compressions and breathing. Do not lift your fingers from the correct spot when you give the breaths and do not interrupt the rhythm of compressions to give the breaths.

5. Check for the baby's pulse after 30 seconds, and if there is still no pulse continue *five* compressions to *one* breath. It is essential to continue the chest compressions and breathing until help arrives. If possible, work in a team so you don't exhaust yourself.

6. When the heart begins to beat on its own, continue breathing for the baby as described above in "Breathing For an Infant" until he begins to breathe on his own. *Never* use chest compressions on a baby whose heart is beating.

How to Help a Choking Child (over one year of age)

1. If the child is coughing or gagging, encourage him to continue. He may cough the object up without your assistance.

2. If the child cannot cough up the object and is having difficulty breathing have someone *call for an ambulance*.

3. If the child is coughing weakly or makes a high-pitched sound while breathing, OR, if the child cannot speak, breathe, or cough or if he clutches one or both hands to his throat in the universal sign of distress, these are signals that his airway is partially or completely blocked. *Administer first aid as follows:*

4. Use a modified Heimlich maneuver: If the child is conscious, stand behind the child, wrap your arms around his waist, bring the fist of one hand against his stomach between his naval and his rib cage, and, covering the fist

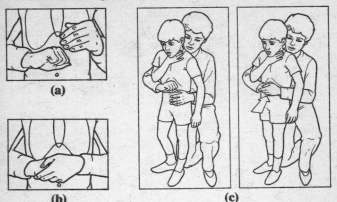

(a) Location for abdominal thrusts.
(b) Hand placement for abdominal thrusts.
(c) Pull upward and toward yourself.

with the palm of the other hand, pull in upward and toward yourself. Pull in with force, but not so hard you hurt the child.

If the child is unconscious, place the child on the floor or on the table, and stand or kneel at the child's feet. Place the heel of one hand on the abdomen between the naval and the rib cage and place the second hand on top of the first. Press upward with quick thrusts (6 to 19 may be necessary).

5. If the object does not come out, repeat until the object is dislodged.

Breathing For a Child

1. Before starting artificial respiration, try to rouse the child by shaking and pinching him and calling his name. If he does not respond in ten seconds, *call for an ambulance immediately*.

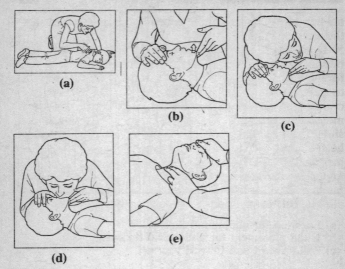

(a)

(b)

(c)

(e)

(d)

(a) Check for unresponsiveness. If he does not respond in 10 seconds, call for help immediately.
(b) With one hand on the child's forehead and two fingers under his chin, tilt the head back to open the airway.
(c) Check for breathlessness.
(d) Open the child's mouth, pinch his nose shut with the thumb and index finger, cover his mouth with yours to make a tight seal.
(e) Using two fingertips, check for the pulse on the side of the neck closer to you.

2. Position the child on his back on a hard surface.
3. With one hand on the child's forehead and two fingers under his chin, gently tilt his head back. This will open the airway. Do not completely close his mouth. You may have to clear out his mouth using your fingers or a cloth.
4. Look to see if the child's chest is moving; listen for sounds of breath; feel for air on your cheek. If there is

no sign of breathing in five seconds, begin breathing for the child.

5. Open the child's mouth, pinch his nose shut with the thumb and index finger of the hand that is holding his forehead and, covering the child's mouth with your mouth to make a tight seal, give him two slow breaths. Keep the child's chin lifted with two fingers of the other hand. Remove your mouth to get each breath. The child's chest should move up and down. You may have to tilt the child's head slightly farther back to open the airway. After readjusting the head, check again to see if the child is breathing. If the chest still does not move up and down, his air passage is blocked and you need to clear it as described above in "How to Help a Choking Child."

6. Check for a pulse at the neck to the side of the windpipe. Take up to ten seconds to feel the pulse—it is easy to miss. Check for the pulse on the side of the neck closer to you. Use your fingertips, not your thumb.

7. If there is a pulse but the child still is not breathing, continue giving him artificial respiration at the rate of one breath every four seconds or fifteen breaths a minute. Maintain the correct head position so the airway is open. Check to see if the child has resumed breathing on his own. Keep breathing for the child until help arrives or until he can breathe by himself.

8. If there is no pulse, begin stimulating circulation with chest compressions (see below).

Stimulating Circulation For a Child Whose Heart Has Stopped

1. Begin with artificial respiration as described above. You should already have called for an ambulance. After breathing, check for the child's pulse carefully at the neck

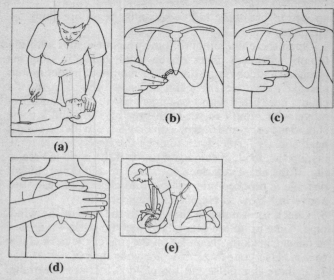

(a)

(b)

(c)

(d)

(e)

(a) Position child on his back and tilt his head back.

(b) Find compression position. Using middle finger, locate lower edge of the child's rib cage on the side closer to you.

(c) Slide middle finger up to notch at end of sternum. Measure the width of two fingers above the notch.

(d) Place the heel of your hand on the sternum directly above this point.

(e) Pushing straight down from your shoulder blade, give five compressions, followed by one breath. Hold the child's head in place with the other hand.

to the side of the windpipe. Take up to ten seconds to feel the pulse—it is easy to miss.

2. If there is no pulse, position the child on his back on a firm surface and tilt his head back. His head must be level with his heart.

3. To find the correct spot for compressions, locate the notch at the tip of the child's sternum and then measure the width of two fingers above the notch. This is the spot you will compress to stimulate circulation.

4. With the heel of your hand compress the child's sternum an inch to an inch-and-a-half *five* times in succession and then give the child *one* breath of air as described above in "Breathing For a Child." Each minute you should be giving the child a total of *fifteen* cycles of *five* compressions to *one* breath or about *eighty to one hundred* compressions and *fifteen to twenty* breaths per minute. Push straight down from your shoulder. Use the other hand to hold the child's head in place so the airway is open. Work quickly as you alternate compressions and breathing. It is easier, if possible, to work in a team, with one person doing the compressions and one doing the breathing.

5. Check for the child's pulse after a minute, and if there is still no pulse continue five compressions to one breath. It is essential to continue the chest compressions and breathing until help arrives.

6. When the heart begins to beat on its own, continue breathing for the child as described above in "Breathing For a Child" until he begins to breathe on his own. *Never* use chest compressions on a child whose heart is beating.

Bites and Stings

Treatment for bites from animals

1. If the child's skin is broken by a bite from an animal or person, *call your physician at once*.

2. If the child is bleeding, follow the directions for treatment of "Bleeding" below.

3. Wash the bitten area with soap and water and cover it with a clean dressing or cloth until a doctor can examine it.

Treatment for bites from poisonous snakes and spiders

1. *Get the child to a doctor as soon as possible.*
2. Until you can get medical help, keep the child as inert as possible and be especially sure that he doesn't move the bitten part. The less the child moves, the less venom will spread through his body.
3. If the child stops breathing before he can be seen by a doctor, use artificial respiration: "Breathing For An Infant" or "Breathing For a Child" above.
4. Do not put ice or cold compresses on a snake bite.
5. While waiting for medical help, lie the child down, elevate his feet, and keep him lightly covered.

Treatment for tick bites

1. Using a tweezers, carefully pull the tick off. Make sure you get the head. Dispose of the tick by burning it or flushing it down the toilet.
2. If the child develops a skin rash and/or flu-like symptoms, *get medical help at once.*

Treatment for bee stings

1. *If you know the child is seriously allergic to certain bees or if he shows a serious reaction such as considerable swelling or difficulty breathing, call for medical help at once.* If the child stops breathing, use artificial respiration: See "Breathing For an Infant" or "Breathing For a Child" above.
2. For less serious reactions, try to pull the stinger out with a tweezers, but do not squeeze or rub the raised area.
3. Wash the area with soap and water and apply ice or cold water.

Apply pressure to stop bleeding using sterile gauze, if possible.

Treatment for jellyfish stings

1. Wash the area with salt water.
2. Remove as many of the stinging tentacles as you can with a towel or stick (do not use your bare hands).
3. If available pour household vinegar over the area that was stung.
4. If the child has serious pain or develops a skin rash, *take him to an emergency room at once*.
5. If the pain is only mild, make a paste of baking soda and water and cover the area that was stung.

Bleeding

Treatment for superficial cuts and abrasions

1. If the cut is to the eye, if the cut seems very deep, if the child has a bleeding disorder, if the skin is hanging in flaps, if you suspect there might be internal injury (for example, the child has been hit hard by a large or fast moving object), or if there is a great deal of dirt rubbed into the cut, *take the child to an emergency room at once*.
2. For less serious cuts and scrapes, first wash the area under running water to get rid of loose dirt.

3. Carefully wash the cut or scrape with a mild soap and warm water. Pat it dry using sterile gauze.

4. Leave large superficial scrapes uncovered and keep the area dry; adhesive bandages are good for small cuts; a clean dressing held in place by adhesive tape works well for slightly deeper scrapes.

Treatment for more serious cuts and wounds

A. Direct Pressure

1. If there is serious blood flow from any part of the child's body, if the skin is hanging in flaps, if the cut is to the eye or seems deep, *call an ambulance or take the child to an emergency room at once.* Use the treatments outlined below only until you can get medical help.

2. Try to stop the bleeding by applying direct pressure with your hand. If possible, use sterile gauze or at least a clean absorbent cloth. When the gauze becomes soaked with blood, apply another gauze pad on top—do not remove the lower pad.

3. Raise the wounded limb higher than the heart.

4. When the blood flow stops, bandage the area carefully (make sure the bandage does not cut off all blood supply to the limb). Lie the child down and keep him lightly covered until medical help arrives.

5. If the pressure from direct pressure does not slow down the bleeding in five minutes, apply a tourniquet—see below.

B. Tourniquet

1. A tourniquet should be used *only* as a last resort when the two methods described above have failed to stop the bleeding. Because a tourniquet can cut off circulation so

completely that irreparable damage can be done to the leg or arm, you should not use one unless the child's life will be threatened by further heavy loss of blood. *You should already have called for an ambulance*.

2. The tourniquet can be a belt, strap, or strip of cloth at least two inches wide. It should be applied around the leg or arm approximately one-half inch above the wound.

3. Tighten the tourniquet until the bleeding stops, but no tighter. Do not cover the tourniquet but leave it in place unless a doctor tells you to do otherwise.

4. Note the precise time when you fixed the tourniquet in place. Get the child to an emergency room as quickly as possible. Until the child receives medical help, lay him down and keep him lightly covered.

Treatment for internal bleeding

1. If your child has suffered any kind of hard blow to the torso, the stomach or the chest (for example, in a car accident, by falling seriously off a bike, by getting hit by a falling tree), you should be alert to the possibility of internal bleeding. There may be no external signs or there may be dark red vomit, bright red blood or a tarry-looking substance in the child's stools, or foamy blood coughed up from the lungs.

2. If any of these signs are present or if you have any reason to suspect internal bleeding, *call for medical help at once*. The child should not drink anything.

3. While you are waiting for an ambulance, lie the child down on his side, keep his legs elevated, and keep him covered lightly.

4. If the child is not breathing well, try lifting his head and shoulders. If breathing stops, use artificial respiration: see "Breathing For an Infant" or "Breathing For a Child" above.

Burns

Burns By Fire or Heat: First and Second Degree

1. In a first-degree burn, the skin is red.

In a second-degree burn, the skin is red and blistered.

In a third-degree burn, the skin is broken, and is black, white, or gray in color and looks charred. Third-degree burns require different treatment than first- and second-degree burns: see below.

2. If a child's clothes are flaming, smother the fire by placing the child on the ground and wrapping him in a rug, towel, heavy blanket, or by lying down quickly on top of him. If the clothes are smoldering or soaked in boiling liquid but not flaming, carefully remove them, but *do not peel off clothes that are adhering directly to your child's skin*.

3. For first- and second-degree burns, place the burned skin in cold water for about ten minutes. If you cannot immerse the burned area, cover it with cold compresses.

4. When the child feels more comfortable, dry the burned area gently and cover it loosely with a clean lint-free dressing, such as household aluminum foil.

5. *Never* put butter, spray, or ointments on burned skin. Do not break the blisters.

Burns by Fire or Heat: Third Degree

Important: A third-degree burn is a serious medical condition and requires medical attention. Call for an ambulance at once or get the child immediately to an emergency room.

1. In a third-degree burn, the skin is broken and is black, white, or gray in color and looks charred.

2. If your child has a third-degree burn, *never* immerse the burned area in cold water or put ice or butter on it,

Wrap him in a rug or blanket to smother flames...

never peel back the broken skin or remove burned fragments of clothing, *never* dab at the burn with cloth or cotton.

3. Lay the child down with the burned area elevated higher than the heart. Keep him lightly covered.

4. For third-degree burns on the face, make a cool compress by wrapping a bag of ice in a towel and apply it very gently to the burned area. Do not wet the burn. Burns on other parts of the body should be covered lightly with a dry, clean, lint-free dressing or cloth.

...or lie down quickly on top of him.

5. If the child stops breathing, use artificial respiration: see "Breathing for an Infant" or "Breathing For a Child" above.

Skin Burns by Chemicals

1. Wash the chemical off the skin with as much cool water as you can get quickly. Use a shower or garden hose, if possible, or douse the child with copious amounts of water for about ten minutes.
2. Once the child is in the shower, take off all clothing that has come in contact with the chemical.
3. If the burn looks serious, bring the child to an emergency room or call for an ambulance.
4. Dry the child and cover the burned area with a clean, dry, lint-free cloth or a clean dressing.
5. Lie the child down on his back or side, elevate his feet, and keep him lightly covered.

Choking

See "How to Help a Choking Infant" and "How to Help a Choking Child" above in the CPR section.

Drowning

1. Call for help at once.
2. In getting a child out of deep water, it is safest for you to remain on land if possible and to reach out an arm, leg, towel, pole, or similar object to him while you hold onto a stationary object on shore. If you must wade or swim out to him, try to have a buoy or similar floating object to throw to him so you can tow him safely in to shore, rather than have him grab onto you and risk pulling you under.

Reach out an arm, leg, towel or similar object to the child while you hold a stationary object on shore.

3. If the child is not breathing on his own, begin artificial respiration at once, even starting while you are standing in shallow water: see "Breathing For an Infant" or "Breathing For a Child" above.

4. If you think the child's neck has been injured, arrange for him to be floated onto a support for his neck and back before you take him out of the water.

5. Once the child is breathing on his own, lie him down on his back, keep his head turned to the side and his feet elevated, and keep him lightly covered until medical help arrives.

6. If the child has been unconscious even for a moment or has stopped breathing for any amount of time however short, he should be seen by a doctor as soon as possible.

Electrical Shock

1. Never touch a child directly when he is in contact with an electrical current.

2. Try to break the current by turning off the power source, pulling out the plug, or pulling the wire away.

3. If you cannot break the current, stand on a dry surface such as a rubber mat or pile of newspapers and, using a nonmetallic object such as a broomstick, board, rolled-

up newspaper, or chair leg, try to get your child away from the power source. Either push your child away from the wire, outlet, whatever, or try to knock the wire away from the child. It may be necessary to fashion a kind of lasso out of rope and loop it around one of your child's limbs in order to drag him away.

4. If, after being removed from the power source, the child is not breathing, begin artificial respiration: see "Breathing For an Infant" or "Breathing For a Child" above. If your child has suffered burns, see "Burns by Fire or Heat" above.

5. After the child begins breathing on his own and after you have treated the burns, call for medical help. Lie the child down on his back, keep his head turned to the side and his feet elevated, and keep him lightly covered until medical help arrives.

Head Injuries—Concussion

1. If a child receives any kind of serious blow to the head or if a child becomes unconscious even for a moment from a head injury, he should be seen promptly by a doctor. In the case of a serious head injury or concussion, the child may show some of these symptoms: difficulty breathing, discharge of blood or clear fluid from the ears, mouth, or nose, vomiting, convulsions, prolonged unconsciousness.

2. If your child shows any of these symptoms, *call for an ambulance at once*. Do not transport the child to a hospital yourself unless absolutely necessary.

3. Until the ambulance arrives, lie the child down on his back, support his neck and shoulders with a pillow, and gently roll him onto his side to allow fluids to flow freely out of his mouth.

4. If the child stops breathing, begin artificial respiration: see "Breathing For an Infant" or "Breathing For a Child" above.

Poisoning

For any kind of poisoning:

1. Call a poison control center and the child's doctor at once. Do not rely on antidotes printed on the labels of toxic products.
2. Try to find out *exactly* what the child ingested and how much. Save the container and a sample of the child's vomit.
3. Do not induce vomiting until instructed to do so by an expert. For poisonings by corrosive acids, alkalis, and petroleum products (see below), vomiting will make the situation worse.
4. Always have on hand *syrup of ipecac*. This is what you use to induce vomiting for most poisonings. If available *activated charcoal* is also useful in adsorbing poisons in the gastrointestinal tract.
5. Do not offer water to a child who is unconscious.
6. If the child stops breathing, begin artificial respiration: see "Breathing For an Infant" or "Breathing For a Child" above.

Poisonings by Acid, Alkali, and Petroleum Products

Important: Before attempting any home remedies, contact your child's doctor and a poison control center. Use these instructions only if you cannot get medical help.
1. Examples of poisonous substances in this category are: carbolic acid, ammonia, drain cleaner, lime, bleach, nitric, sulfuric and hydrochloric acids, battery acids, lac-

quer thinner, gasoline, floor and furniture polish,
kerosene, lye, oven cleaner.
2. Symptoms of acid and alkali poisonings include:
   —burns or stains around the lips and mouth
   —a feeling of burning in the mouth and throat
   —cramps and diarrhea with blood in it

   Symptoms of petroleum poisonings include:
   —coughing and gagging
   —internal burning sensations
   —the smell of petroleum on the breath
   —coma

3. Treatment for poisoning:
   —do not induce vomiting.
   —give the child one or two glasses of milk to coat the
stomach, but *only if he is conscious*. If there is no milk
available, give him water.
   —lie the child down on his side, loosen his clothing,
elevate his feet, and keep him lightly covered until help
arrives.

Poisonings by Harmful Household Products, Foods, or Drugs That Do Not Contain Acid, Alkali, or Petroleum

Important: Before attempting any home remedies, contact your child's doctor and a poison control center. Use these instructions only if you cannot get medical help.
1. Examples of poisonous substances in this category are:
aspirin, after-shave lotion, alcohol, antifreeze, chlordane,
deodorants, hair dye, paint, perfumes, sun block, and sun
oils.
2. Symptoms of these poisonings may include:
   —nausea
   —drowsiness and/or dizziness
   —slurring of the speech

—failure of physical coordination
—skin that is cold and damp to the touch
—thirst
—convulsions
3. Treatment for poisoning:

—give the child a glass or two of water but *only if he is conscious*.

—induce vomiting (only if the child has not already vomited up the substance) by giving the child syrup of ipecac. Dosage: one teaspoon for an infant; one tablespoon for a child between one and ten years; two tablespoons for a child over ten. After the child swallows the ipecac give six to eight ounces of water.

—if no vomiting occurs in twenty minutes, repeat the correct dose of ipecac and give another glass of water. *Do not give any more ipecac after the second dose*.

—if no vomiting occurs after the second dose, try tickling the back of the child's throat using a spoon handle or your finger.

—when the child does vomit, place his head down between his legs or hold a small child on your knee with his head facing down. Save a sample of the vomit.

—after the child has vomited, have him drink a mixture of water and activated charcoal (about one tablespoon per 17½ pounds of body weight mixed with one cup of water).

—lie the child down on his side, loosen his clothing, elevate his feet and keep him lightly covered until help arrives.

Poisonings by Inhaled Fumes or Gases

Important: Contact your child's doctor and a poison control center as soon as you have removed your child from the source of the poisonous fumes or gases.
1. Examples of poisons in this category are: exhaust gases from automobiles or engines of heavy equipment, heavy smoke from poisonous chemicals, paint fumes.

2. Symptoms of inhaled fume poisonings include:
   —irritation to eyes, nose, mouth, throat
   —coughing
   —headaches
   —difficulty breathing
   —dizziness
   —convulsions and unconsciousness
3. Treatment for poisoning:
   —get the child away from the poisonous fume source and into clean and fresh air. Avoid breathing in the fumes as you remove the child.
   —if the child is not breathing, begin artificial respiration: see "Breathing For an Infant" or "Breathing For a Child" above.
   —once the child is breathing on his own, lie him down on his side, loosen his clothing, elevate his feet, and keep him lightly covered until help arrives.

Poisonings by Ingestion of Harmful Plants

Important: Before attempting any home remedies, contact your child's doctor and a poison control center. Use these instructions only if you cannot get medical help.
1. See Chapter 3 for a list of common house and garden plants that are poisonous.
2. Symptoms of plant poisonings may include:
   —nausea and vomiting
   —dizziness
   —feeling of burning in the mouth and throat
   —stomach pain
   —rapid pulse
   —difficulty breathing
   —skin rashes
3. Treatment for plant poisoning:
   —give the child a glass or two of water but *only if he is conscious.*

—induce vomiting (only if the child has not already vomited up the substance) by giving the child syrup of ipecac. Dosage: one teaspoon for an infant; one tablespoon for a child between one and ten years; two tablespoons for a child over ten. After the child swallows the ipecac give six to eight ounces of water.

—if no vomiting occurs in twenty minutes, repeat the correct dose of ipecac and give another glass of water. *Do not give any more ipecac after the second dose*.

—if no vomiting occurs after the second dose, try tickling the back of the child's throat using a spoon handle or your finger.

—when the child does vomit, place his head down between his legs or hold a small child on your knee with his head facing down. Save a sample of the vomit.

—after the child has vomited, have him drink a mixture of water and activated charcoal (about one tablespoon per 17½ pounds of body weight mixed with one cup of water).

—lie the child down on his side, loosen his clothing, elevate his feet, and keep him lightly covered until help arrives.

Poisonings by Touching Harmful Plants

Important: If the child has an extreme reaction, contact the child's doctor at once.
1. Examples of poisonous plants in this category are: poison ivy, poison oak, poison sumac, poisonwood trees.
2. Symptoms of poisonings by skin contact with these plants include:
    —burning and itching sensation on the skin
    —skin rash, sometimes with blisters and swelling
    —headaches
    —fever
3. Treatment for skin poisoning:
    —remove any clothing that has come in contact with the harmful plant.

—wash the affected skin with soap and water and then dab it with rubbing alcohol.

—cover the affected skin area with calamine lotion.

—in extreme cases, the child may stop breathing or become unconscious. If the child is not breathing, begin artificial respiration: see ''Breathing For an Infant'' or ''Breathing For a Child'' above.

—wash the child's clothes at least twice, making sure to keep them separate from other laundry.

Index

About the Author

David Laskin is the father of a daughter and twin girls. He is the author of *Getting into Advertising* (Ballantine, 1986), *Parents Book for New Fathers* (Ballantine, 1988), and *Eastern Islands* (Facts on File, 1990). He has also written articles on parenting, travel, home entertainment, and manners that have appeared in *Esquire* magazine, *Travel & Leisure*, the *New York Times*, *American Baby*, *Parents* magazine, *Redbook*, and other publications. He lives outside of New York City with his wife, their growing family, and two large dogs.

Parents® MAGAZINE
READ ALOUD
BOOK CLUB

READING ALOUD—the loving, personal gift for you and your child to share.

Children's reading experts agree . . . reading aloud offers the easiest, most effective way to turn your child into a lifelong reader. And, it's as much fun for you as it is for your child.

Easy access to a variety of such important "first" books (read-aloud books) has presented a major problem for busy parents. And a challenge that *Parents* Magazine was well suited to undertake.

The result—a book club that can be your child's *first club*. A club for sharing and reading aloud. An early reading habit to last a lifetime, with books designed, created and published solely for this purpose. *Parents* Magazine Read Aloud Book Club.

If you're a concerned parent, and would like more information about our club and your free gift, just fill in the coupon below, and mail it in.

Parents® MAGAZINE
READ ALOUD BOOK CLUB

1 PARENTS CIRCLE
P.O. BOX 10264
DES MOINES, IA 50380-0264

Yes, I would like to receive free information on *Parents* Magazine Read Aloud Book Club.

To find out how to receive free gifts along with membership, simply fill out this coupon and mail it today. There's no risk or obligation.

YOUR NAME   (PLEASE PRINT)

ADDRESS   APT. NO.

CITY   STATE   ZIP

BRINGING UP BABY

A series of practical baby care and family living guides developed with the staff of *Parents Magazine*. Explains both the *whys* and *how-to's* of infant care.